SINS OF
HENRY COUNTY

AFTER TWO WRONGFUL MURDER CONVICTIONS & THE DEATH
OF JERRY BANKS, A 35-YEAR-OLD COLD CASE IS REINVESTIGATED

By
CHARLES L. SARGENT

REVIEWS

UNIVERSITY OF GEORGIA SCHOOL OF LAW

Perversion of Justice: A Double Murder in Henry County Re-examined
By: Donald E. Wilkes, Jr., Professor of Law
Thursday, October 18, 2012
Charles L. Sargent, a retired Georgia businessman, has written a book that everyone should read and none should forget. It is (amazingly) the first book ever written about one of the most shocking perversions of criminal justice in the history of this state. Sins of Henry County (Published, in 2012) tells the true but terrifying and tragic story of an innocent man who was railroaded by corrupt police and sent to Georgia's death row, and of the brutal double-murder for which he was framed–execution-style killings which remain unsolved after nearly 40 years.
Sins of Henry County admirably recounts both a horrifying perversion of criminal justice and an immense human tragedy
Sins of Henry County vividly impresses upon us the profundity of something a Georgia judge said nearly a century ago: "One of the most dangerous manifestations of evil is the lawlessness of the ministers of the law." For this reason and many others, Sins of Henry County is an essential book. Buy it. Read it. And never forget it.
Donald E. Wilkes, Jr.
For the complete copy: Perversion of Justice - Digital Commons @ Georgia Law

Amazon Reviews

A miscarriage of justice and a call to action..., June 22, 2012
By: purplecat
Two words describe this book: riveting, and scary.
... Banks was innocent and was being framed, but nobody knew why or by whom. Anyone who did know was either in on it, or too scared to talk. Read this book if you want to find out. Charles Sargent did a staggering amount of research before writing this book, but if you're expecting dry nonfiction, think again. Sargent is a natural storyteller, and in his words the Banks story unfolds like he is talking to you over a cup of coffee at his kitchen table. The murders of Marvin King and Melanie Ann Hartsfield went unsolved, but not before, an innocent man's life was destroyed. This is a cold case that needs to be reopened.
There are still people walking free, holding their heads up in what passes for society in Henry County, with blood on their hands.

✠ ✠ ✠

Finally, justice? June 12, 2012
By: juanhorn –
This book is very intriguing. It was hard to believe that the law enforcement agencies involved could be so incompetent, but it was a time of "good ole boy justice" in the south. If a person had enough money or power, they were above the law and could get away with almost anything, even murder. Many people were too afraid of the consequences of questioning the illegal actions of those in power, and as a result just kept their mouths shut. Charles Sargent is to be commended for his bravery and tenacity in researching the facts of this case ... The real murderer was never caught and convicted. We can only hope that there is enough public out-cry to force the case to be re-opened so that justice can finally be served.

⊕ ⊕ ⊕

A sad but true story of injustice, July 1, 2012
By: Walter T. Yancey
I think it is a MUST READ for anyone who remembers that terrible day. The book clearly makes the case that Banks was wrongfully accused and convicted. However, it leaves us still hopelessly asking the question as to WHY Melanie and Marvin were murdered. To this day - I still think of them often and I loved them dearly. It's a sad story but I'm glad I read it...

⊕ ⊕ ⊕

REVIEWS OF BOOKS RECENTLY WRITTEN BY ATLANTA SOUTHSIDE AUTHORS

By: Forrest W. Schultz, June 26, 2012
... the author concludes that there was a conspiracy which caused the infamous 1974 double murder in Henry County and which covered it up and which framed Jerry Banks. The various interlocking complexities and questions are too tedious to even list, let alone analyze, in a review. One thing I can say for sure, though, is that if you like murder mysteries and if you are concerned about justice, you should read this book. Investigations should be made to determine the truth and then the appropriate actions should be taken.

Copyright © 2012 Charles L. Sargent

All rights reserved. No part of this book may be used or reproduced in any manner whatsoever without written permission of the Publisher.

This book is a work of Non-fiction. All characters and their names, incidents, and dialogues are drawn from the author's investigation and from court records and they are real. None of the names have been changed to protect anyone.

Published by the Independent Writer's Gallery in partnership with CreateSpace, an Amazon Company

ISBN-13: 978-1475004939

ISBN-10: 1475004931

Library of Congress 1-647990791

Published and Distributed by the Independent Writer's Gallery

in partnership with CreateSpace, an Amazon Company

IWG

Front cover picture Source: Wikipedia, Old Sparky

Book cover design: By Charles L. Sargent

DEDICATION

To my wife, Cheryl:

Everything in this book is what I wanted to know since late 1974, but for decades I was too afraid to ask questions. As I entered my 60s, I started asking because it was time to tell the Jerry Banks story. I'm so sorry for putting you through the many years of worry and absolute fear of the people who were involved in the wrongful conviction and death of an innocent man, as well as those involved in the 35-year-old unsolved execution of two people. I feel too guilty and ashamed to even bring up what you have gone through. I thank you for your silent support and understanding that this was something I had to finish.

To all Dyslexics:

To all those who are dyslexic yet are filled with many stories in their hearts and mind. To all of you as well as others who are too afraid to step out and express yourself. I feel like I was a participant in a special Olympic event in which I have won. I have been held back all of my life. I was rejected from college because I could not pass the Regents' Exam which every student must pass after their core curriculum. That was Georgia law; it was a road-block for people who were born with dyslexia. It was discriminatory. After failing on my second try, even though I was passing my classes, I was not allowed to choose a major. I cannot imagine anything after the Regents' that would be impossible for a dyslexic to overcome to earn a degree.

I know even if I were to have earned a Masters degree, I would still be a dyslexic. Dyslexia interferes by slowing down the speed of reading *and writing. Dyslexia also causes difficulty in spelling, none of which reflects intelligence or IQ. I have more common sense and a higher IQ than average. I have managed to build a small business that grossed over $700,000 a year income up until 9-11.*

If you have stories to tell, you can do it, too. Start by joining a local writer's group as I did or form your own group. Attend classes at your local school or college. Find a good local editor. Your written words are your microphone to the world.

CONTENTS

Dedication	vii
Table of Contents	ix
Preface	xi
Acknowledgment	xiii
In Memoriam	xv

PART I : I Will Never Forget a Man I Never Knew	1
CHAPTER 1. My Journey Begins	3
CHAPTER 2. Jerry's Journey Begins	9
CHAPTER 3. The Setting	19
CHAPTER 4. My Research and Investigation	23
CHAPTER 5. The Murder Investigation and Arrest	39
CHAPTER 6. Georgia v. Banks I	45

PART II : Another Dog and Pony Show	53
CHAPTER 7. The Bullpen	55
CHAPTER 8. A Bond Between Two Strangers	59
CHAPTER 9. Georgia v. Banks II	65
CHAPTER 10. The 2nd Verdict	97
CHAPTER 11. Relevant Facts and Dates	109

PART III : Exhibits   119
STATE EXHIBITS   121
MAPS AND PHOTOGRAPHS   123
THE TIME LINE   135

PART IV : Pro Bono Lawyers   141
CHAPTER 12. Answered Prayers   143
CHAPTER 13. The December 22 Hearing   159
CHAPTER 14. The Ace   165
CHAPTER 15. Exculpatory Evidence   171
CHAPTER 16. Clayton County Detectives   179

PART V : A Time to Die   183
CHAPTER 17. Does Our System Work?   185
CHAPTER 18. Jerry Banks' Journey Ends   189
CHAPTER 19. $12 Million Civil Action   195
CHAPTER 20. Jimmy, Jimmy   201

PART VI : A Man Separated from His Soul   209
CHAPTER 21. A Misty Morning   211
CHAPTER 22. What Did He Know and When Did He Know It   217
CHAPTER 23. A Conspiracy in Henry County   223
CHAPTER 24. D. A. Tommy Floyd   229
CHAPTER 25. My Journey's End   241
EPILOGUE. My Promise to Jerry Banks   253
LIST OF MAIN CHARACTERS   261

PREFACE

This story has been in my heart and mind for 35 years before I could bring myself to realize two things. The first ... no one on the face of this Earth was going to tell this story if I didn't. The second ... I was not going to my grave allowing Jerry Banks' story to remain untold, even if my grave came sooner than later.

The Jerry Banks story started in McDonough, Georgia, in November, 1974. Jerry Banks, a 23-year-old black man, borrowed his brother's shotgun for the very first time on November 7, 1974, and took his little puppy on their first training mission. On this adventure, his dog discovered two bodies lying under a red bedspread. A white 35-year-old male high-school teacher and a 19-year-old female student had been executed with a 12-gauge shotgun.

Hal Gulliver, editor of the Atlanta Constitution wrote, "Jerry Banks was tried twice, convicted twice and sentenced to die [in the electric chair] twice."

The day Jerry Banks was arrested I knew he was an innocent man who was going to be framed. How I knew this is another book in itself. I carried Jerry's story with me all of those years waiting for the TRUTH to be told. What became apparent to me ... I was not the only person deathly afraid of Sheriff Jimmy Glass and what one phone call, could do. I pass this man daily because he lives up the road from my house, coming and going as though he has no sins.

In 2005, I started my six-year research and investigation as low key as possible. The problem for me, all of the files on Georgia v. Banks were in the courthouse basement and the majority of the principals were law enforcement officers, some still working. I researched and studied with a fine tooth comb legal documentations, actual court testimony from two trials, hearings for extraordinary motions, crime-scene photographs, and decisions from the Georgia Supreme Court as well as the United States Supreme Court.

The years of work brought me to know many great people in this story. I interviewed retired police officers, three of Jerry Banks' five lawyers, several judges, our District Attorney, and agents from the GBI and FBI, all of whom were most informative yet totally surprised by my inquiries. One of the greatest joys of my life was my conversations with Jerry Banks' younger brother Perry Banks and Jerry Banks Jr., particularly getting their blessings on this book. The end result of my six years of research will show clearly there are unrepentant sins in Henry County, Georgia.

Stepping out openly from 2005 thru 2011 and asking questions about the biggest murder case and trial in the history of Henry County, Georgia, was a task that changed my life, even how I took my nightly medicine in the dark.

The bottom line seemed to always be the same: "Why are you writing this book?" My first response was much like George Mallory's when asked why he wanted to climb Mt. Everest ... "Because it's there!" But to be polite, I always followed up with "Because somebody needs to."

The most difficult task was interviewing the families of the two murder victims whose lives have settled, and in the last 35 years managed to have distanced them from their pain. I managed to resurface the pain, forcing it upon them out of my own needs. But in the end, as they gave me their blessings as well, I gave them my promise to find those who murdered their loved ones.

Sargent, Charles. January 20, 2012, composed in my soon-to-be uncluttered office.

ACKNOWLEDGMENTS

"The Righteous, and the Wise, and their Works, are in the Hands of God:" (Ecc 9:1)

To Henry County citizens:

Sins of Henry County, is in no way a blanket indictment on Henry County or the citizens past or present. Nevertheless, the good thing about the acknowledgement of sins is that it is the first step in reconciliation, forgiveness, and salvation. Righteous ... sometimes ... wise, very! And this story has been inspired by God.

There are sins in Henry County as you will learn from reading the Jerry Banks story. The sins I chose to write about belong to a select few people within this county. Henry County had more than serious problems within their law enforcement community in years past but it did not end there. For me personally, the Jerry Banks story and how it was handled fortunately caused this problem to surface. A sin can be something you commit. It can be something that you willfully do, but also it can be due to something you fail to do ... fail to act, fail to speak out, fail to help a fellow human being, fail to "do unto another as you would have another do unto you."

When Jerry Banks was falsely convicted, twice, the people of Henry County had not sinned in the eyes of God. There were good people in Henry County who saw the injustice in Jerry Banks' murder trial and acknowledged it. There were others who saw the serious problems within our law-enforcement community, and they acted accordingly. These good people came from the heart of Henry County. More great people are in this story than not, honorable people who came to the aid of Jerry Banks. At the same time, many things were left unsaid and other's sins were forgotten in order to protect an honorable county. If it means revisiting these sins, in order to tell Jerry Banks' story, then so be it. There are people from Henry County who still live here today who may need more than our prayers.

TO MY EDITOR:

Thanks to a very special person, my editor who chose to remain anonymous, for agreeing to edit a dyslexic's book. I cannot think of a more difficult task in the field of writing. She has unscrambled my eggs into a very nice omelet.

We could write a book on this book's journey alone. You have done much more than edit my work. Your skills have been so valuable in organizing my fragmented thoughts and rearranging the three-dimensional time periods of the Jerry Banks story. Without your help, none of Jerry Banks' story would have been told.

IN MEMORIAM
Robert A. (Bob) Maddox

You'll read about my good friend, Bob, in this story. The last time I spoke with him in the summer of 2010, I was telling him about this book, hoping he could fill in between some of the old lines. I would have given a "Gold Guinea" to know all of what he knew. I could tell he remembered me but his mind had faded as far as Sheriff Jimmy Glass was concerned. I didn't press the issue, not wanting to waste our time on bad memories.

I will always remember the advice he gave me so many years ago ..."Son, you are an entrepreneur, a person who is willing to take a risk in business. But remember one thing ... you can't sit around waiting for things to happen; you must make things happen."

Robert A. Maddox was the single greatest influence in my life, by far more than my own father, and he will truly be missed by many. My friend passed away the winter of 2010. May God bless him and keep him at His side.

PART I:
I WILL NEVER FORGET A MAN I NEVER KNEW

CHAPTER 1

My Journey Begins

DECEMBER 11, 1974:

This day was a mark in time for me. It was the day I heard Jerry Banks was arrested in a month-old murder case. **See Figure1: Jerry Banks**. It was truly a day neither of us would forget. On November 7, 1974, Jerry Banks, a simple black man from rural Henry County, was caught up in one of the most overlooked and unjust crimes in Georgia. He served six years on death row for a double murder he did not commit, and subsequently his ultimate death left more than blood on the hands of county officials.

    Jerry Banks would never enjoy another day on this earth, and I would never forget a man I never knew. On that December day, when I heard the news that Jerry Banks had been charged with two murders, I felt his innocence in such a profound way. There could not have been another person living on Earth who needed God's help, more that day than Jerry Banks, and I felt as though God sent him to me. It was as though Jerry Banks was crying out, and God chose to connect him with me at that moment. The insight into another man's soul and the connection by a higher power was given to me in an instant. Although we were 25 miles apart, this man could have been on the other side of the world.

At that moment, it was as though I had been put on notice, like a witness to come forward. But there lies the rub. What did I know? I didn't know anything. And I had not seen anything. However, I did accept this notice, because I knew something wasn't right about this arrest. All I had were my gut feelings, and they were just that, and nothing else ... my feelings. For three decades, I have been living with those same feelings.

As of 1981, these were the only details about this case of which I had any knowledge:

1. At some time in November of 1974, a friend of mine informed me about a male high-school teacher from Jonesboro, Georgia, and a female student who were murdered over the Henry County line in Stockbridge, Georgia.
2. December 11, Jerry Banks was arrested, and the police discovered the murder weapon, a shotgun, in his home.
3. Shortly after, in January 1975, Jerry Banks was found guilty and sentenced to die in Georgia's electric chair.
4. Early in 1978, Cindy Glazier, a newspaper reporter from a local Clayton or Henry County newspaper, came forward with evidence that Jerry Banks might not have received a fair trial.
5. In 1981, I remember hearing the news that Jerry Banks was dead. From then on, I learned bits and pieces, mainly scuttlebutt that I picked up here and there.

Everything I tell you from here on is what I have always wanted to know since the murders happened. For decades, I was so afraid to ask any questions. I didn't know much, but I knew this was not a subject I wanted to bring up around town.

Over the years, I tried to think of how often these people were on my mind, in terms of, let's say, how many days a week or a month. Years ago I could have come up with an answer for that. Today, looking back, I cannot tell you the last time they were not on my mind. I have always felt this must be divine intervention, my destiny, because it would never let me go.

Other than Jerry Banks, the two murder victims from my hometown of Jonesboro, Georgia, weighed on my mind. The murders and everything I managed to learn about the case were truly shocking. Back in the 70s, it appeared this case was not handled in a normal manner.

Looking back now, time shows the lack of consideration for the murder victims was appalling. The way this murder case was handled was even more astonishing.

Who am I? I am a white male born in 1948. Who I am is not important at this time.

Who am I to tell this story? Well, there is a good chance you have never heard of this story. And it is possible you have heard of it, and if so, you think you know what happened. It has been many years, and no one else has bothered to come forward to find out what really happened. That is where I come in. I am now an expert on Georgia v. Banks. With that being said, it is important to understand a decent person would not make fun of a cripple or anyone with a disability of any kind. It is my place to let you know I am dyslexic. You may very well spot things in my writing that may cause you to think I'm not a writer. Whatever, please don't turn away from this story because of my disability.

⁂ ⁂ ⁂

1970's:

I returned home from Vietnam in January 1969. During the early 70s, a time in which things were supposed to have changed in this country, I began a career in construction. I wanted to take advantage of every remaining moment in my life and make the best of it.

Around 1973, I had befriended, or had been befriended by, one of Clayton County's most respected businessmen in the State of Georgia, who was on the board of directors of several of the oldest banks on the south side of Atlanta. Robert A. (Bob) Maddox was as honest as any man I have ever known. He was, in my personal opinion, the finest man ever to wear shoe leather.

The day I became a part of Jerry Banks' story was back in November 1974. My first recollection of the murders was when Mr. Maddox and I were driving down Rock Quarry Road. He pointed out a side road, an old dirt road I believe, and he said. "That's where they found the bodies of those two people." He could tell by the look on my face, this was news to me. "They were murdered," he said.

That seriously grabbed my attention. "They were a male high-school teacher and a female student." The one point of our discussion that rang out the loudest, and still does after all these years, was the way he remarked "They just happened to find the two bodies over the county line." The victims were from Clayton County. He shook his head and remarked, "What a coincidence it was to find them there." Those words didn't mean anything to me at the time, but I never forgot them, and years later these words were still on my mind.

Thanksgiving break of 1974 was nearing at Clayton Jr. College. There were discussions and details talked about at school as well as all over town. It was at the Jr. College I first learned the 19-year-old female victim was Melanie Ann Hartsfield, a student there as well. **See Figure 2: Melanie Ann Hartsfield**. One cold night, several students were standing in the parking lot after classes talking about how horrible her death was. The word "shotgun" created flashes of images as my mind tried to process the unimaginable events this young lady went through at the end of her life. The other victim, Marvin King, was a 38-year-old band director from Jonesboro High-school. **See Figure 3: Marvin W. King**. With all the work on my plate and going to college nights, I didn't have time to stay on top of the details.

I do remember a lot of talk about the victims' age difference. Then again, there was talk from people, who said they knew the teacher,

My Journey Begins

who said his life style was a bit higher than the average teacher's salary would allow. The word "drugs" did enter more than one conversation, but you know how people talk. I, on the other hand, believe until you know the whole story, you don't know the whole story.

As you will later see and understand there was never the first indication that Marvin King acted inappropriately that day or did anything other than try to help Melanie Hartsfield.

By the end of 1975, I had accepted the fact that Jerry Banks was going to be put to death. This bothered me more than you'll ever know. During this period of my life, I was busy building houses and working long hours and coming home at all hours of the night. Five years went by and I had been under the impression Jerry Banks was either awaiting his death or had already been executed. Working hard and taking care of my family, building a future as a contractor, along with attending college occupied my every moment. During this long period, long before my investigation, I had not read or heard about any details that led up to the fact that Jerry Banks received a second trial. This is not to say I had ever forgotten or quit caring about Jerry.

One thing needs to be understood. During the time this story was unfolding, the only story that occupied the news media was the Atlanta child murders and Wayne Williams. This story was covered worldwide, while Jerry Banks slipped through the cracks.

As time moved on, I was full of regrets whenever I happened to think of Jerry. But life went on in both Clayton and Henry County. One evening during the spring of 1978, the Jerry Banks murder trial was back in the news on Channel 2, WSB TV out of Atlanta, and they were saying a young newspaper reporter, by the name of Cindy Glazier, had evidence Jerry Banks may not have received a fair trial. That was the last I heard about the case until I received the news that Jerry Banks was dead in March of 1981.

❖ ❖ ❖

I will give you facts from years of research of court documents from the local courts to the Georgia and United States Supreme

Courts, my interviews and my investigation. There are five things I hope my work here will accomplish. I will also give you my queries, thoughts, beliefs, and my reasoning. Here is a list of things I wish to shed light on, and I hope you will be able to formulate your own opinion from reading my results.

1. I first set out to show anyone with an ounce of intelligence that Jerry Banks was innocent and let them figure out if Jerry Banks was framed. In doing so, the King and Hartsfield families would find themselves back to zero not knowing who killed their loved ones. However, by the end of this story they will be better informed than they were three decades ago.
2. I want to shed enough light on the real reasons the case ended the way it did, and why I feel a double homicide case was allowed to be put to rest in such a manner that it insured the King/Hartsfield murders would never be truly solved.
3. I want to give others a reason to ask the same questions I have been waking up to for over 35 years. Who were Marvin King and Melanie Ann Hartsfield, and what did they do to be murdered?
4. I want my readers, at some point, to understand why I feel it to be so important to pray for the sins of some people within Henry County as well for the soul of Jerry Banks.
5. I want to show the importance of listening to nagging thoughts within us that we sometimes ignore.

It was not my intention to go beyond these five issues. But if you feel by the end of this book that you have a better understanding of the issues, along with an idea of who might have been responsible for the murders, then that will be a bonus.

You will need to takes notes, study the time line, and go over the testimony carefully. Then make up your own mind. During the reading of Jerry Banks' story, you will ask your own questions. This is not because I failed to think about them; it is because I reached a point where I became too afraid to turn over any more stones.

CHAPTER 2

Jerry's Journey Begins

Jerry Banks and I were about the same age. At the time, I didn't think we honestly had anything else in common. But he was the one who occupied my thoughts the most. The teacher and/or the student may have been involved in something or had knowledge of the activities of others that got both of them murdered. They were not robbed or at the wrong place at the wrong time or anything like that. They were murdered, execution style. My heart went out for them and their families as well. And I have never believed they were murdered by Banks, therefore I have always been of the opinion that if I understood why Jerry Banks was railroaded, I would have a better understanding of why King and Hartsfield were murdered.

Jerry Banks weighed heavily on my heart and stayed in my mind for all these years because he was at the wrong place at the wrong time and his suffering was significant. As far as I was concerned all three were victims and they would be on my mind forever.

Jerry Banks died on March 29, 1981, with a broken heart. What was the cause of death? The coroner said a bullet to the chest at very close range. But that does not begin to describe what really killed him. The tragedy of his death was overshadowed by the circumstances that led up to it.

There was a brief moment, from the time Jerry was shot until he hit the floor. He didn't have much time. This brief moment would have been the single most important time in his life. I have heard people say, your life passes before you as you die.

It is my prayer that Jerry Banks made his peace with God earlier that day, if not, hopefully before he hit the floor.

⊕ ⊕ ⊕

Going back in time, to the day of the murders, the following would be Jerry Banks' story as he would have remembered it based on my understanding, from my years of research.

On Thursday, November 7, 1974, Jerry Banks, a 23-year-old man, lived with his wife, Virginia, and three beautiful children ... five-year-old Jerry Jr., three-year-old Ed, and Felicia, a newborn. They lived outside of Stockbridge, Georgia, off of Rock Quarry Road, which ran between Hwy. 42 and Interstate 75 just south of Atlanta.

That day started out as normal for Jerry as it would for any other normal family. The mornings around any home with three small children would always be special. The kids would wake up much too early, and then come running into their parents' room and crawling in bed with them. Those moments and the things they would say were as special to the children as they were to their mom and dad. They had things to tell ... how much they loved them, and what they were going to do that day. Sometimes they just lay there on top of their parents, not saying a word, just holding them. Jerry Banks had a family and just because they were black doesn't mean they were not normal.

Jerry Banks had plans to go rabbit hunting that day, a pleasant November day, the beginning of the holidays. He and his two brothers, Ludie (older) and Perry (younger) were raised without a father. Their Uncle Roy was a significant part of their life. He had taught them how to fish and hunt. However, their mother served as mother and father.

Some will say Jerry Banks got up early and went hunting all day, the day of the murders. "I remember him leaving that morning with the gun and he was gone all day," said Jerry Banks Jr. in 2009.

It was an old broken Stevens Arms, break-top single-barrel shotgun. It worked but it was held together with a lot of black electrical tape. **See Figure 4: Stephens Arms break-top shotgun**. It was also said, Jerry Banks first went over to help his neighbour, Mrs. Slaughter. He was an unemployed truck driver and had been showing up at her house every morning, to work on some chores around her place. Jerry Banks said he worked until lunch that day and spent the remainder of the day rabbit hunting.

A little before 5:00 p.m., Jerry Banks had followed his puppy to an old dirt roadbed that ran off Rock Quarry Road. **See Figure 5: Aerial Photograph of Crime scene**. The puppy found some blood on the ground, fresh blood and a lot of it about 200 yards from Rock Quarry road. That was not normal. Jerry looked around, suddenly becoming extremely nervous at the sight of two pools of blood side by side. The pool of blood to the right showed drag marks leading toward the woods. As he looked in that direction, he noticed the dog had wandered off into those woods. He called for the dog, but could see she was over in a heavy pine thicket. Jerry Banks could tell she had found something else. As he worked his way through the heavy brush, over to her, he saw two bodies covered with a red bedspread.

Slowly and carefully pulling the spread away, he noticed a man and a young girl, both white, faces down. They had both been shot in their mid-section and also in the head.

Jerry Banks hurried up to the paved-top and tried to flag down several cars. Out in the country back then, there wasn't a lot of traffic on that road. Every now and then a car would drive by but they didn't want to stop. Mr. Banks figured when white folks

Sins of Henry County

see a black man with a shotgun flagging down cars, they tend to be concerned. He did manage to get one to stop, but when he told the driver of the two bodies in the woods, he said he didn't want to get involved. Soon another white man stopped. Jerry explained again what was going on. "Would you please call the police and have them come out here." The driver agreed but as he drove away, Jerry felt he wasn't going to call anybody.

Jerry Banks continued flagging cars, if and when they came by. He managed to get another driver to stop. This man was concerned; he was thinking there may have been a hunting accident. Jerry Banks again explained about finding the bodies and asked if he would please call the police. "And tell them, I'll be here waiting…tell them, I'll be standing out here…by the road," he yelled as the driver drove away. This driver said he would be right back. That's what the other one said earlier. Jerry stood there with his puppy and his shotgun until about 6:00 p.m. when the passerby returned with his son.

They stood there and waited with Jerry and his little dog. He told Jerry he had called the Henry County Sheriff's Office and it was sending an officer. They talked there along the side of the paved-top; none went up into the woods. Jerry Banks didn't want the police to miss him and drive on by. The man gave his name as Andrew Eberhardt and it was nice of him to help Jerry.

About 6:10 or 6:15 p.m. Detective (Charles Richard) Dick Barnes of the Henry County Sheriff's arrived. He had been told a black man hunting in the woods had found two bodies. Jerry was the only black man dressed in hunting clothes and standing by the road with a shotgun under his arm, so he introduced himself to Jerry as being Officer Barnes. Jerry Banks explained who he was and that he was the one who flagged down the man who called the police.

"What do you have?"

"There are two bodies back here, in the woods."

"Show me."

The two of them walked up the unused roadbed about 200 yards where Mr. Banks showed him the pools of blood. **See Figure 6: State Exhibit #2: The Two Pools of Blood.**

Jerry's Journey Begins

"My dog found this first."

Officer Barnes stood there, looked down and nodded his head, then looked up and around as if to say, what else?

Jerry Banks then pointed, "This way."

They walked over a hundred feet back into an area that was all grown over with weeds and into a pine thicket.

In a short time, the place was covered with authorities from both Henry and Clayton Counties. The Clayton County police had been putting out a missing person's call over several counties via the radio. Melanie's ring was removed by Henry County police and her full name was in her Jonesboro High School ring. Therefore the Henry County police answered the radio call.

They uncovered the bodies and took lots of pictures. They were walking around everywhere, pulling tape measurements from here and there. They appeared to be measuring everything from the pools of blood, determined to be the spot where the victims were shot. They looked at some fresh tire tracks. A car had driven in to the old road bed, stopped and just turned around and drove out, back to Rock Quarry Road. There was no car found there and there were no other car tracks at the murder scene.

The sun sets early in November, so the passerby sent his son back home to get a lantern, so the police could see what they were doing.

There Jerry Banks was standing in the middle of a double homicide investigation all evening and into the night with his shotgun and his puppy and the police just kept working. Every now and then someone would ask if he was the one who found the bodies. That was all. At the time, he didn't think about it, but not one of those officers ever asked for his gun, never asked to let them put it away, never checked to see if it had been fired or if there was a spent round in the chamber. They never asked what kind of shells he had. They never asked him to sit in the back of their car. All of the things a trained officer should have performed were overlooked. I cannot imagine a group of police officers conducting a murder investigation while letting someone walk around the crime scene with a shotgun.

Sins of Henry County

Jerry Banks was still there well into the night. They were all just trying to help. That was what Jerry Banks wanted to do, help.

Even the passerby and his son were still there late into the night. When Sheriff Jimmy Glass arrived, the motorist made a point to introduce himself to him. "I'm the fellow who called, Andy Eberhardt, and I'm married to Jo Austin." It was something to that general effect and he shook hands with Sheriff Glass. As he talked to the Sheriff, Mr. Eberhardt made the comment "You went to school with my wife." The Sheriff did seem to recall her and after a bit more small talk, Sheriff Glass then excused himself. "I appreciate it but I've got a speaking engagement; I need to run."

Sometime between 9:30 p.m. to 10:00 p.m. the bodies were removed from the scene and taken away. Jerry Banks walked on home. It wasn't much of a walk. He was less than a mile from home.

⚜ ⚜ ⚜

At midnight Officer Barnes knocked on Mr. Banks' door, and asked him to come with them down to their office to give a statement. After sitting around all night at one of the detective's desk, they finally took his statement in the early morning hours of how he found the bodies. They were asking him to tell them what, when and where about this, that and the other. It was all about what Jerry Banks had found. At that time, nobody accused him of anything. He was only a witness.

Jerry Banks was returned home at 5 o'clock in the morning on November 8, 1974. There is no record of which officer or officers drove Jerry Banks home that morning. The police had already returned to the crime scene an hour earlier, at 4:00 a.m. that same morning. The exact time was never pinned down by Lead Detective Phillip Howard, but he stated in court he found the first shotgun shell casing between 7:00 a.m. and 9:00 a.m., then four or five minutes later Detective Ted Ray found the second shotgun shell.

Jerry's Journey Begins

Officer Dick Barnes testified in court that he returned to Jerry Banks' house several days later on Sunday, November 10, to pick up the gun so they could run comparison ballistic tests. Jerry Banks wasn't worried. He knew that was just one of those things the police did in their investigations. But, Jerry Banks' brother, Perry, and Jerry's wife were worried. They had a bad feeling about the whole thing.

Well, the Sheriff's Office came back again, on December 5, 1974. They told Jerry Banks they needed his shotgun again, because the shells they found at the crime scene had come from his gun.

Jerry Banks told them, "No way! There's got to be a mistake."

Sgt. Tommy Floyd read Jerry his rights and loaded him into their car; Jerry Banks explained to them that he didn't have the gun with him.

"It is over at Perry's house. It is his gun. I only borrowed it."

Sgt. Tommy Floyd and Detective Paul Robbins escorted Jerry Banks to his brother's house and then to their office for more questioning.

Another unknown fact to this day is who, when and why was this alleged murder weapon returned to Perry Banks after the November 10th borrowing of the gun? It would have been sometime after the test-firing by Lead Detective Howard. Again no one could remember this from November 10th until the end of January, the time of the first trial. I learned early in this case, when they cannot remember something, they are hiding something. Make note of this.

After stopping by his brother's house, Jerry Banks was taken down to the Sheriff's Office for more questions. This time the questions were different.

Well, the police didn't let any grass grow under their feet. On December 11, Sgt. Tommy Floyd was right back at Jerry's door with a warrant for his arrest.

Perry Banks tried to help by saying he hunted that area with that same gun and those shell casings found at the murder scene could have been there from weeks or months earlier.

The truth of the matter is, with those three shotgun shells found at the scene of the murders, his efforts were a waste of time. If Jerry Banks had been hunting all day with the Twelve Disciples, those people would still have found him guilty of those murders.

Everybody was just trying to get the police off his back. Jerry Banks even told them, he had loaned the shotgun to another man and said he must have killed those folks. He was scared, just plain scared. This is the closest he would ever get to Hell on earth. He had plenty of reasons to be scared.

Anybody who ever grew up in these parts knew there were certain people you just didn't mess with. And it didn't matter which color you were.

⊕ ⊕ ⊕

The only items missing from the murder scene were both of the victims' car keys. Mr. King's wallet was first said to be missing, but Jerry Banks had been questioned about it and he told them he took the man's wallet from his pocket and threw it in the woods and there was no money in it.

On December 12, Jerry Banks was taken from the jail to the crime scene to find the wallet. After arriving there he told them a different story about the wallet. Jerry Banks told another version when he stated he picked the wallet up from the ground near all the blood.

On December 13th, an attorney was appointed to represent Jerry Banks and that ended their questioning.

⊕ ⊕ ⊕

At this point, there's not a lot to tell you. Jerry Banks did not know any more than the above facts. He was being charged with murdering the two people he tried to help.

Jerry Banks' hopes were that, being he hadn't done anything wrong, all of this would be fixed and he would go back home. On the other hand, the police and the District Attorney Ed McGarity were convinced Jerry Banks killed those people and it did not appear to be any way to change their minds.

Was that Jerry Banks' story or his journey? Was it the truth? The best I can discern from talking to his family, friends, and attorneys, it indeed was the truth. That was pretty much the way he would have remembered the events of that day.

CHAPTER 3

The Setting

Jonesboro is the county seat of Clayton County, which is about 30 miles south of Atlanta. If you have ever seen or read <u>Gone with the Wind</u>, you have been introduced. The main highway running through Clayton County and the City of Jonesboro is called Tara Blvd. Jonesboro was the location for Margaret Mitchell's fictional Tara Plantation. This road was mentioned in her book and it will bring you into McDonough square where Henry County courthouse and old jail house still sit today. There have been stories going around that Margaret Mitchell lived in Atlanta but often visited her grandmother or great aunt, who lived in the Clayton County area; and then she was inspired to place her plantation (Tara) in this location. I have been to this precise home site and walked around the grounds, which still had foundations intact from multiple slave quarters.

There is another landmark nearby, the home of U.S. Senator Herman Talmadge. This old plantation site is said to be the house used in the opening scene of the movie. I had the pleasure of meeting Mrs. Talmadge at the home of Bob Maddox. While Senator Talmadge was no longer a resident in this stately home, I visited with, and did manage to perform a small task or two for, Mrs. Betty Talmadge, during her U.S. Senate campaign, and in its day, this was a most beautiful home.

According to and told by historians: On August 31, 1864, General William T. Sherman put the small city of Jonesboro, Georgia, on the map by trying to take it off the map. Sherman and his army of over 60,000 men collected to the east of Jonesboro and stood by until August 25, when he and his men moved in from three sides. If Sherman could take Jonesboro, he would be able to cut off the much-needed supplies to the Confederate troops. Jonesboro was a tremendously beneficial rail hub, which supplied Gen. John Bell Hood, who was defending Atlanta. By General Sherman moving in to cut off the rail lines, this thoroughly severed Hood's supply lines, and it drew General Hood away from Atlanta, where he was outnumbered and defeated.

The Battle of Jonesboro was the final battle of the Atlanta Campaign, and it caused the besieged city of Atlanta to fall into Union hands. The capture of Atlanta greatly aided the re-election of President Lincoln.

McDonough is the county seat of Henry County, adjacent to Clayton County, and the town square is one of the most impressive in the state of Georgia. The town square has been home to many festivals throughout the years and presently is the home of the *Geranium Festival,* which is held every spring and draws a large crowd every year. In the recent past McDonough was still a sleepy town. On Saturday evenings during the summer the square was closed off to traffic so locals and visitors could sit out and listen to music well into the night, as children ran about playing and dancing. Back in the 1800s, McDonough was a stage-coach stop on the route from New York to New Orleans.

McDonough was the home of the company once known as Snapper Lawn Mower, the largest manufacturer in town. Henry County is the home of the Atlanta Motor Speedway owned by Bruton Smith, located next door to McDonough in the city of Hampton.

Jonesboro was our home from 1972 to 1989, when we moved to McDonough. At the time, McDonough was the best-kept secret in Georgia. For the most part, the fine people here are true Southerners through and through and the newcomers are truly welcomed.

The Setting

I cannot say there has ever been anything which happened in Henry County that would have been covered by the evening news like the Jerry Banks story. The sad thing about that story is remarkably few people know what truly happened and it was the biggest murder case in the history of Henry County, Georgia.

I love Henry County and the people who live here and I realize there are many people who have never heard of Jerry Banks.

Jerry Banks of course has never left my thoughts. There are people who remember the Jerry Banks case, but they have no idea of the hidden truth behind the story.

CHAPTER 4

My Research and Investigation

FROM 1989 TO 2002:

Moving to McDonough jump-started my interest in getting the answers I have always needed. I started to ask questions in the black community through contacts in the construction field, friends I had working relations with going back 20 years, people I trusted. Their thinking was the same as mine ... Jerry Banks got a raw deal. But no one knew anything; for every question I had for them, they had two for me.

FROM 2002 TO 2005:

I called everybody but the Pope. I tried to talk to the local newspapers. I called the Henry County detectives and there was no record of any such case and if I am not mistaken, there was no Cold Case Division. I called television stations in Atlanta and the majors in New York, Unsolved Mysteries, America's Most Wanted, Nancy Grace, and even Greta Van Susteren. I either could not get past the front desk or I didn't have enough information to develop the interest of their producers. I did manage to communicate with Dale Russell from Channel 5, The Fox Station in Atlanta. He was and still is their chief crime investigator.

The first time we talked, he listened to my story about how I believed this, that and the other about the Jerry Banks case, and boy did I feel like a fool. I didn't know enough of the facts to be talking about Jerry Banks. I had not begun my research yet. Here I was, calling all over the country, with nothing more than my compassion for another human being, who I didn't know, and armed with only the faith that God had given me this task.

Mr. Russell explained there was no way he could justify the research dollars needed to investigate a 35-year-old cold case that (according to me) had already been solved in two separate trials, both rendering guilty verdicts and handing down death sentences.

Although I felt like a crackpot, my resolve returned. I was sure that if and when I completed my investigation, he would change his mind.

However, at that time, I realized just how right he was. I could not get anyone to look into this case. By talking with Dale Russell I learned I would not be able to approach this as an outsider, as an observer. It would have to be the other way around. The only way I could uncover the truth about the Jerry Banks case would be to get my hands on the court records of State v. Banks.

2006 AND 2007:

It was during this time that I picked up my writing again and before I knew it, something else came over me. In my wildest dreams, even from the beginning in 1974, I never planned to write this book. Then out of the blue, I told myself, *"I'm going to do this"*.

It also helped that I was finishing up my first book about my life and all my memories. Originally, I wrote it for my family, thinking I wanted to be remembered as more than just an 8x10 on the wall. No, it is not published yet; I'm still here and I'm sure I'll have a few more memories. The title is guarded at this time. I haven't decided if I'm putting my name on this book yet!

The other project gave me the feeling that I could do the research and write "Jerry's Book." The only problem was I had not worked out the part that was going to keep me alive! I have been interested in writing all my life. Since I was a child, I have always had stories in my head. I always dreamed of writing. I could only dream of it though, because I was as dyslexic as a wheelbarrow and still can't spell my way out of a wet paper sack. I now have two things it takes. I still have stories in my head, and I have Microsoft Word with Spell Check. This is one story that will certainly quiet the un-rested souls which have become a part of my life. There was only one problem. I had written every thought in my head, expressed every feeling in my heart and I had stated every fact I knew and I had less than 60 pages. I had come to the point in my life where I needed to either step out and find the truth about Jerry's case and the answers to the many questions running through my mind or forget this project forever.

MAY OF 2008:

My open but guarded research began. I had called every Banks in the phone book and found no one related to Jerry or anyone who knew of him or his remaining family. I thought it would be smart to start out by meeting with the locals at Shiloh Baptist Church in McDonough. This is the largest black church around town. I called ahead and made an appointment to see a lady name Willy.

With a bit of nervousness mixed with overwhelming pride, I entered through the office and surveyed the area. My eyes fixed on a little sweet-looking lady, who turned out to be Willy. I introduced myself by name and as a writer. Oh Lord, what a way to start out, standing there in a church lying. Well ... at what point do you genuinely become a writer?

She was a sweet lady and highly enjoyable to meet.

She was and still is a historian of sorts in the black community. She indeed remembered Jerry Banks and the first thing she said, "He was the man rabbit hunting". I enjoyed a pleasant conversation and she was more than helpful. She gave me the name of a 90-year-old lady by the name of Mrs. Hambrick.

Mrs. Willy said, "She was a friend of Jerry Banks. If there is anybody who can help, it would be her."

After talking with her, I was afraid there were not going to be any young people around who were going to be of any help, and the people who would be the most useful were going to be so old that they might not remember anything, they had moved, or were dead. That however was not the case. Well, that was my first interview and I must say it went okay.

From the church, I walked several blocks to the courthouse. That was something I had dreamed of for so many years and there I was finally doing it. As I cut across the landscaping of the town square, through the hundred-year-old oak trees, standing there also for over a hundred years, I could see the old courthouse, without any prejudice of the good or evil that passed through its chambers. My thoughts faded back to the days when Jerry Banks was in her care and a tremendous sense of sadness came over me. As I passed through the security system, I knew, other than my responsibilities to my family, I was about to launch the most substantial commitment of my life. I wanted to uncover dark mysteries, which could easily get me killed. This was not going to be a game. These were real lives, real people involved in something extremely serious.

I asked the security guards for directions to the Records Department. As I walked in and stood there, I could see two large counters, and I walked up to the first available lady and asked how one would go about looking at old records.

She asked, "Civil or Criminal?"

"Oh, this would be criminal," I said.

She pointed to the other counter. I stepped back and then realized someone had gone to the trouble of putting signs on the front of each counter, "Civil" and "Criminal." I thought to myself, *"I'm going to have to be more observant if I'm going to find the needle in this haystack."*

Now standing at the proper counter, in a low voice, I asked Mrs. Price "Who can help me with some old court records?"

"I can help you. What was the name on the trial?"

I said softy, "Jerry Banks."

"I'm sorry, I didn't hear that," she replied.
I leaned over and repeated in a quiet voice, "Jerry Banks."
"What was the year?" she asked.
"The early 70s," I said.
"Oh, I'll have to get someone else for that. I haven't been here that long. I can't help with anything going that far back. "
A few minutes later another extremely likeable lady walked up behind the counter.
"What was the name of the person on trial?" she asked.
Again with the lean, I repeated, "Jerry Banks."
Well if you could have seen her face. It was a wonder I didn't hightail it right out of there, but I hung in there. *"I can do this,"* I told myself.
She said. "Oh me, that must have been 1975, maybe 1974."
"Yes, that's right." I wish I could describe the look on her face. It was a look somewhere between "Oh Hell, what is this guy up to," and "Oh Hell, all that stuff is in the archives and that means it's down in the basement."
I asked her. "Do you remember that case?"
"Oh, yes." she laughed. "I was only 18 at the time; that was the biggest trial we ever had in Henry County."
"Then there were a lot of records involved?" I asked.
"That's right. It will take us awhile. Give us a week."
"That's fine. I'll check back with you. If you need help carrying it up, I'll help."
She shook her head, "No, that's okay. What is your name and phone number?"
I gave her my number. She wrote it down and looked up at me for my name. I remained silent. She started to ask again; then with another look on her face, she nodded her head and kindly said, "Okay, that's fine." I think there was a strange look on my face that time.
I got a call the next day from Mrs. Price.
"We got the records you wanted."
I could not wait to get back down to the courthouse to get my hands on those records. My wife went with me; wild horses could not have held her back. We had to park across the street in the

courthouse parking, which gave us a lengthy walk. On the way, she complained she could not keep up. I was walking too fast for her.

"Just move your feet twice as fast, you'll catch up." I stopped as soon as I realized what I had said. "I have been waiting a long time for this. This day is going to be the day, the day I get the answers I have been asking for since 1974. This will be a lot like opening someone's casket. I'm nervous."

Inside the courthouse, the ladies led us to a separate, glassed-in room, where we could be seen at all times. There it was ... an old cardboard file box with a string which secured the lid and covered with decades of dust. **See Figure7: Court Documents: Georgia v. Banks.** I saw "Jerry Banks" written on the face of the box, and I froze as I realized just how serious his situation was. It all came to light. When you have a file of a murder case with your name on it in the Superior Courthouse ... well, it doesn't get any more serious than that. I felt Jerry's fears come over me for a brief moment. My chest tightened as my breathing labored. I could see myself for a split second sitting in that courtroom living my worst nightmare. At the same time I felt Jerry's pain, his suffering and his fears. Suddenly the simple act of swallowing was no longer an involuntary action. Inside this box was a real person who once lived and died. A person whose life was swept up into a dustpan and discarded like yesterday's trash from the sidewalk.

I could hardly move the box myself. I carried it as though it were a casket over to another desk by the front window with a view of the large oak trees filling the square. Very gently, I removed the old dusty cardboard lid. I opened it up, along with 35 years of hidden sins. There it was, all that was left of Jerry Banks, a man and the truth about his life.

I realized in all those court records was the truth which had been withheld from all but a decided few in the legal system. As far as the rest of the people of Henry County and the rest of the world, they didn't have thoughts, concerns, compassion, and anger going on in their heads over this case.

I told my wife, "There are sins in this box and they belong to people who still live here in Henry County and they need to be addressed."

Standing there, I asked for a blessing of this journey as I placed the dusty lid to one side. There was no room for another file to fit in that box. I found myself passing my hand completely across all the files, letting my fingers slowly touch each as though they were keys on a piano. A name came to me out of the past, and I knew it would be found in these files. At that moment my mind shifted to years past.

I looked back, to traveled roads that took me places, with total amazement of how I survived in some cases. Yet these roads were as different as night and day, in purpose and time, yet they were as interconnected as a crossword puzzle of my life. These roads I will cover in another book but let me share a few here.

GOING BACK TO 1974:

A gentleman well-known in the restaurant business in Clayton County during the 1970s and 80s hired me to construct a secret room above his restaurant. This required a new, much steeper roof, a new floor system in place of the ceiling and the main requirement was not the hidden stairway but my silence.

This person was a high-roller and the purpose of this secret room was for a group of heavy gamblers. Names were mentioned. The one that stood out the most was that of a law-enforcement official from Henry County. Several of his comments about this group back then and other comments over the years, from others in a tri-county area have described to me the existence of an underground society. He described the group as being large in size, people with money and people who loved to party. He told me of their many rendezvous at Lake Lanier where everyone in the group who owned a house-boat tied all of their boats together like a floating island for a three-day party of drinking, gambling and, with his quick up-and-down movement of his eye-brows, "a whole lot more."

BACK TO THE OLD DUSTY BOX:

Standing before the court documents, the words of wisdom given to me by my dear friend Bob Maddox came back to me as my mind traveled down another road.

IN THE MID 70'S:

I had brought up this name (of a law-enforcement official), in a conversation about heavy gambling. This was several years after the period in which Bob pointed out the crime scene as we were riding through Stockbridge.

Bob was concerned and told me, "Son, you need to stay away from him." He got real close, eye to eye.

"Do you hear what I'm telling you? There's nothing that man will not do ... Do you understand what I'm telling you? Not... one...thing! There...is...not...one thing that man...will not do. Do you understand?"

"Yes, Sir ... Yes, Sir." I had no idea what my friend was telling me at the time.

BACK TO COURTHOUSE IN 2008:

Bob Maddox's statement was the single most important conversation which convinced me that I was on the right track. I always had a feeling, if this official were in charge when Jerry Banks was arrested, he would be the center of my investigation.

Mrs. Price agreed to make a copy of State v. Banks, which I picked up a few days later, and I have never slowed down since. For a month or so, I regularly visited the courthouse reading and tape recording various documents.

After studying these documents harder and longer than anything I had ever studied in my life, I began to see things that drew me to them, which led me to a very different conclusion than either jury.

I then knew all of the principals. I knew who I was dealing with. I knew who to avoid. I knew who would like to kill me but, best of all, I also knew the ones from whom I could get the truth and talk with freely.

⚜ ⚜ ⚜

I wasted no time in calling retired Judge, now Attorney Alex Crumbley. My visit with him came early in my investigation but what I found out during this exchange was not learned in this actual case until six years after the murders. I cannot reveal this information now. It is my goal to reconstruct this case and relay this story to you in the same order in which the two juries, the public, the newspapers and Jerry Banks' lawyers were made privy to the facts of the case. Not always in the order as the events happened but always in the order as they became public knowledge. There will be times when I clear up puzzling events or statements for you by drawing from information that I have learned.

As an added bonus, I will then share with you, the two juries (if they are still around), the public, the newspapers, and a lot of people with blood on their hands, all that I have learned.

✥ ✥ ✥

I was getting up in age, 60 to be spot on. I had come to the end of my building career which included over a million square feet of Day's Inn Motels, apartments, office buildings, and over 100 homes in the South Atlanta area and the largest ceramic tile company on the south side at that time. With the major slow-down in the home building industry which I saw coming around 2006, I retired in 2008. Considering how the rest of the country was faring, we were blessed to be able to keep our home and get by much better than others.

BACK TO THE INVESTIGATION 2008:

As I stated previously, I had begun my open but guarded research in May of 2008. The first thing I noticed as I read every word of the **State v. Banks** was that the prosecution, which consisted of District Attorneys Mr. Ed McGarity and Assistant District Attorney Mr. Harold Craig, called nine witnesses, and Defense Attorney Hudson John Myers called only two. This was more than troubling to me; it was insane.

The second thing I noticed was the name of a law-enforcement official involved in this case, and I knew then all my suspicions for 35 plus years were about to be confirmed. Back when I first learned Jerry had been arrested, I did not know this officer was involved. I knew of him, just from scuttlebutt, but I didn't put him in the picture the day I said "my God, he is innocent and they are going to frame him."

Remember Jerry's journey, about what happened the day of the murders, how he found the bodies? Could that have been a story he made up?

When I first read the trial testimony hidden away in that old dusty card-board box stored beneath the floors of our court house for over three decades, things didn't add up. I was confused. I was reading people's statements, learning facts previously unknown to the public at large. I actually asked myself, "My God, did he do it?"

Remember Jerry's story of that day according to family and friends? If you analyze the Sheriff Department's report and the (GBI) Georgia Bureau of Investigation's Georgia Crime Laboratory's test, you see a totally different story:

1. Mr. Banks could not provide a solid alibi.
2. He lied to investigators about the details in which he stole the victim's wallet.
3. There is a strong possibility Mr. Banks never went to Mrs. Slaughter's home that day at anytime.
4. It is possible Jerry Banks could have found the victims parking, as he hunted that area, and decided to rob them when something went horribly wrong. This would have been close to 2:30 p.m.
5. Jerry Banks could have driven the car owned by the murdered victim, Mr. King, when he left the crime scene in order to flee the area much faster. The car was found parked less than a 1/2 of a mile from Jerry's house off Tye Street. This route was on the way home for Jerry.
6. After leaving the scene and returning home, he realized he would be the first person the Sheriff would come looking for. After all, he had already been arrested for killing another man only a few years prior.

7. Jerry Banks could have returned to the murder scene again claiming he just happened to discover the bodies as he then begins to flag down a passing motorist.
8. Jerry Banks could have been under the impression the authorities could not run a ballistic test on shotguns because there was no slug to compare to the marking that would be created as the slug passed through the barrel. Was this why he did not worry about the shells left at the scene? [The understanding that a shotgun and the shotgun shell casings are not traceable by ballistics is dead wrong.]
9. A little known fact: Jerry Banks was given a polygraph examination and the results showed "an area of deception."

With all of this to think about, how could I support Jerry Banks? Hell, I was starting to realize I was 25 miles away at the time of the murders, so what in the hell did I know? Why did I have such strong feelings about his innocence all these years? As I read through the trial transcripts, I felt lost and felt out of my league. Could Jerry Banks be guilty? All sorts of scenarios were running through my head. The more I read the trial records, the more I realized I might be wrong about him. How was I going to write this extraordinary story about injustice?

By 3:30 a.m., I gave up and called it a night. On the way to Mass that morning I told my wife. "There is no way on Earth Jerry Banks was guilty. I'll stake my life on it right here at this red-light, and let God strike me dead if he was guilty."

You have to consider I was up all night!

Quickly I realized, from reading the trial transcripts, I had been indoctrinated the same as two different juries. I had in my possession the transcripts from the two trials in 1975 and an extraordinary motion for a third trial in 1980, along with the decision handed down from the Georgia State Supreme Court in 1980. And then, another motion filed and heard on December 22, 1980. My goal became to not just read but study every single word, over and over.

⊕ ⊕ ⊕

I had never read the first newspaper article about this case. After reading every word of Georgia v. Banks, I found myself at the Georgia Archives, reading every newspaper account from the Atlanta Journal and the Constitution. To the normal eye, they read like any other murder story. It was apparent to me while reading these news accounts, after I had read the testimony and after I was privy to all the evidence presented in court, the press had been given misleading statements before the first trial and all of the testimony could not have been true.

This would account for the lack of concern and the lack of any kind of an outwardly following for Jerry Banks or this case. If the newspapers had been more detailed in their reporting of the testimony given in court, other witnesses not present in court, would have seen the dog and pony show for what it was.

I need to relate to you what I have learned from reading the trial transcripts, the news related micro-film, from talking to friends of Melanie Ann Hartsfield and people who knew and worked with Marvin King. I had the pleasure of meeting and talking with Judge Alex Crumbley. Judge Wade Crumbley and Attorney A. J. "Buddy" Welch, all who helped more than anyone will ever know. I interviewed several retired detectives and deputies from the Henry County Sheriff's Department along with several police officers from Clayton County and Spalding County. This list goes on, a host of other people, including 90-year-old Carrie Hambrick who helped me locate Perry Banks and his best friend "Hardrock."

And last but not least Officer Jerry Banks Jr. from the DeKalb County Police Department. Tears came to my eyes the first time I heard those words. When I first talked to Jerry Banks Jr., I told him how truly proud I was of him and I was sure his father was also, as well as his mother. He went on to tell me he became a police officer because of what happened to his father. "I learned at a very early age what can happen to a man if the right people aren't around to help them." That was a once-in-a-lifetime moment for me. I never got a chance to meet Jerry Banks, but

My Research and Investigation

talking with his son was a most noteworthy experience. I can only say I was covered with emotions.

⸙ ⸙ ⸙

I started putting the word out, to people I could trust, that I was writing a book about Jerry Banks. The first person I told was my wife's best friend. Her exact words were, "Oh, I remember that case. In fact, I have a good friend who was Melanie Hartsfield's close friend."

The next thing I know, I'm talking to Melanie's friend, who actually gave me more information on Marvin King and Melanie than anyone else. The compelling thing here was this lady not only went to Jonesboro High School with Melanie, but this lady also went to work for the Clayton County Police Department in 1973, right out of high school. She worked in the records office. She knew Clayton County's Lead Detective Joe Reynolds and all the others quite well and she knew her records. Detective Reynolds' wife was the leading crime reporter in Atlanta for WSB Television. Unfortunately for me, she had just retired and the two of them moved away as I began this adventure. The Clayton County Police Department was not handling the case because the bodies were found over the county line, but they were working to rule out anyone in their county who might have a motive to kill, such as a jealous wife, a boyfriend, that type of stuff. They never came up with anything.

This lady remembered that the Clayton County police were aware of Marvin King long before his death. He was into a 1960's lifestyle. They said he was a partier. I personally thought that is what we all were supposed to do in the 60's.

⸙ ⸙ ⸙

By this time, Perry and I were talking several times a week, sometimes a day. In reading the court records, I came across two black officers who had been at the crime scene. Perry Banks remembered them and felt I could trust them and he was correct. That gave me a better feeling about coming out of the blue asking questions about such a sensitive matter.

My starting interview with those in the criminal justice system was retired Sgt. Johnny Glover. When I asked if he was the same Glover who was with the Sheriff's Department in 1974, he acknowledged that fact. Then I explained why I called.

He said "I really don't want to talk to you about these matters because, well, I don't know who you are."

All those years had passed and this man was still on guard.

I explained to him how I felt about the Jerry Banks case and the way the case was handled and that my intentions were on Jerry's side.

He opened up a little bit, but said "I can't talk to you on the phone. I just can't do it. We'll have to meet somewhere."

He had some things to do with the grandchildren and we agreed to meet in a public place like the city square at the courthouse. I agreed to call later in the week to set that up. And this was one of the good guys.

As time passed, I had several pleasant conversations with both retired Sgt. Johnny Glover and Detective Charles Tomlinson. Perry Banks had later given me a name of another retired black detective named Bobby Lemon. When Perry mentioned Bobby Lemon, I thought he could help. I did call him.

"I don't have anything to say to you." That was all I heard before he hung up the phone.

There is no way to say there was a connection in any way, but the next morning when I entered the courthouse to finish my investigation, all the files, the dusty old box which held all of Henry County's sins, all the testimony in all the trials and hearings were gone. It had been in the glassed-in viewing room right across the counter in the Records Office for well over a month. It was gone. They were told to put it away, behind the counter in their back office.

"Being they are public records, you have a right to see them, but you can only look at them here at the counter. We cannot let any of those records come up missing."

"Ok, do you need me to carry it out here for you?"

"No, you're not allowed back here. I can't lift the box by myself and there is no one here who can."

"I may be overreacting here, but hell, I can take a hint."

I had been in and out of that room for well over a month and there was never a problem. Now these were exceedingly charming ladies and I am sure they were just following orders from someone else. I could only feel that the ladies in the Records Office received a call from somebody up the ladder. I'm sure I was jumping the gun, but when you are involved in a serious case like this, you start looking over your shoulder.

"If I need anything else, I will get it from Clayton County. Besides, I would rather let everyone around here think my project is closed down."

❖ ❖ ❖

I met many friends and foe of Jerry's during this period of my life. The sweetest ever was Jerry's neighbour back in 1974 and she still lives in the same house today. I call Mrs. Hambrick from time to time because her mind is clear and memory is strong.

"I may be ninety years old," said Carrie May Hambrick, "but I know Jerry came over often with severe pains in his head after prison. He was never the same. They done something to him, and he was very depressed, all the time." She told me several times, "All those years in prison done something to Jerry." The truth is without professional help, no one could ever understand what was going on in Jerry's mind.

2009:

I called retired Detective Paul Robbins at his home here in the McDonough area and asked if he remembered Detective Phillip Howard. He said he did and he last heard he was living in South Carolina but he had not heard from or about him in years.

"Who am I speaking with?" he asked.

I told him. "My name is Charles Sargent and I'm writing a book about Jerry Banks. You remember him and Hartsfield and King. I was just wondering if you still remember anything about that case."

His tone changed as though his past had just caught him. "I lived that case and I'll tell you Jerry Banks was found guilty and that's what he deserved. Now I don't have anything else to say to you."

He hung up as though I had insulted him in some way. This was a law enforcement officer who took two oaths, one to become a law enforcement officer and another one to tell the truth in court. According to Detective Paul Robbins, Jerry Banks got what he deserved.

☖ ☖ ☖

2010:

For the past several years, I worked on the two books at the same time. The lack of physical activity during this period of time caused me to gain too much weight and develop high blood pressure. I needed to go back to work and take care of my body. So I applied at a local Home Depot store. During the mid summer of 2010, The Home Depot hired me as a part-time sales associate. Things have never been the same there since. However, this seriously took away my spare time, when it came to my research. I have spent a great deal of time over the years digging deep and trying to leave no stone unturned. The job offer worked out great. I was able to get a job when there was better than 15% unemployment. And as you will better understand later, if I had not been employed at this particular store, I would have never been able to completely finish Jerry's story.

CHAPTER 5

The Murder Investigation and Arrest

Keep in mind this is as much a documentary of facts as it is a story. The following is a list of facts of the case. Some are related, some not, but all are crucial to making my case.

The Atlanta Journal carried the motto "Covers Dixie like the Dew" since it was established in 1883. Their motto was displayed just under their name. On November 8, 1974, the headlines read "Police Hunt for Male Suspect in Slaying of Teacher and Student." Two large black and white pictures of the victims were displayed just below, two attractive people ending up in an ugly story. **See Figures 2 and 3: Melanie Ann Hartsfield and Marvin W. King**. College student, Melanie Ann Hartsfield's high-school graduation picture showed her attractive smile and a picture of teacher Marvin King, also taken from the same year book, showed a resemblance to John Lennon, with hair more of Paul McCartney. Marvin King played in a local dance band in the Atlanta area. He was an accomplished trumpet player; he could be seen and heard at the Atlanta Braves' opening games, as well as other occasions throughout the year. He played at the election celebration party of governor-elect George Busbee. Marvin King was also a valued member of the Atlanta Symphony Orchestra.

Remember how people judged Marvin King because of his life style being a bit higher than the average school teacher's salary would allow? Well, he worked for it.

In this article, Melanie Hartsfield was described by her friend Melanie Fain as "a good Christian young woman and a family friend and baby sitter for Marvin King's family." Miss Fain had spent Thursday evening at the Hartsfield home and was there around 10:30 p.m. when the family was told their daughter was dead.

"She was the kind of girl who would do anything for anybody; when I was down, she was always willing to make me feel better."

There was a statement in the paper, "An unidentified male was being hunted by Henry County sheriff's deputies Friday in the double shotgun slaying." Further down in this article Captain Howard said "No arrest warrant has been made out for this male suspect. Police believe they know who the man is, but his location was not known Friday."

Lead Detective Phillip S. Howard, from Henry County, then goes on record, "The Georgia Bureau of Investigation has not been called in for assistance in the slaying. I have nine detectives and they are some of the best. If they can't do it, then I'll make different arrangements."

✥ ✥ ✥

The Atlanta Journal and the Atlanta Constitution did not merge until 1982. Both papers were covering this story equally. It was reported on the 10th of November that Officer Randy Rivers, the spokesperson for the Henry County Sheriff's Office, stated there was a witness who saw a man in the area of the crime scene with what appeared to be a shotgun. This man was seen also in the area where Marvin King's car was found several miles away. The newspaper made no mention of the man at the scene being black or white.

The papers also reported that the Henry County Sheriff's Department was looking into the whereabouts of a known man

Marvin King had a strong disagreement with during the summer months. It was also stated this lead proved useless to the authorities when it was discovered he had been out of town. Other witnesses saw two young men hunting that day in the same area driving a yellow car. Lead Detective P. S. Howard reported that their identity was known, but nothing had been done with these men.

After reading all the trial transcripts and comparing them to the newspaper reports in 1974 and 75, somebody was giving misinformation in several areas of this case.

In an article released by the Atlanta papers, based on information given to them again by someone within the Sheriff's Department, the victims' personal belongings were reported stolen, rings and watches and things. That was not true. During the court testimony of the autopsy, both Melanie Ann and Marvin King's watches were with them. Marvin King's watch was still running. Their rings were used to help identify the victims, in Melanie Hartsfield's case her name was on the inside of her Jonesboro High School ring. Marvin King's 1959 University of Georgia ring with his initials (MWK) was also removed at that time. Melanie's pocketbook and Marvin King's eight-track tapes were still in place.

Another fact never made public or brought up in any court proceedings until 1980 was that Marvin King had a 25-caliber handgun in his car that day or the fact that he felt a need to carry a hand gun period. Marvin's hand gun was not stolen during the murder. The day after the murders, they found it on the front seat of his car.

After reading the court documents, there were no items proven to be stolen that day other than the car keys. I will say that Mr. King's wallet was tossed into the woods. There was no money inside of it and there was no evidence to say any was stolen from it.

It was almost like they were laying the ground-work for a motive of robbery to put on Jerry Banks.

They were also releasing statements to the press that were next to impossible. "The bodies were still warm when we arrived at the scene," one spokesman stated in the papers.

The deaths occurred at 2:30 p.m. and the soonest these officers could have examined the bodies would have been 6:15 p.m. to 6:30 p.m. on a cool November evening. The high that day was only 54 with a low of 41 degrees. I'm not sure what percentage of you, have held a person in your arms while that person was dying, but I have. As I held this dying man, I could not release him until I knew his soul was no longer there. I could feel the life slip from him and his soul slowly fade away. I could not release him until after his body temperature felt cold; this did not take an hour in much warmer weather.

Now because these victims were lying on the ground during the month of November for 4 hours, there is no way their bodies would be warm. They were painting a false picture of them finding two murder victims at a scene, in which a black man with a shotgun was still in the area, while the bodies were still warm.

✣ ✣ ✣

On November 15, 1975, the Atlanta newspapers reported there were now six unsolved murders within a close time frame and within less than 50 miles of this crime scene. Here in Henry County we had the murders of two people, which in itself had all the makings of a mystery. Two people from Milledgeville, a father and his young teenage daughter, were brutally murdered only 55 miles or so down the road earlier on the same day during the early morning hours of November 7. The killer from Milledgeville was already identified as a serial killer and had been seen in Stockbridge during the daylight hours of November 7.

Mike Thevis lived in Atlanta and worked with gangsters in pornography and organized-crime with the Gambino crime family. Roger Dean Underhill and Kenneth "Kenny the Jap" Hanna were his associates in everything from hardcore bondage, rape, bestiality and eventually child porn. Thevis' name turned up with the FBI when Kenny Hanna was murdered. The FBI realized Thevis' annual income was over $100 million from illegal pornography. Well, you can see we had some heavy hitters around

The Murder Investigation and Arrest

Metro-Atlanta in those days. During the 1960s and 1970s drugs, sex and murder sold like hot cakes from Miami to Atlanta. It was everywhere. The two victims connected to the notorious Mike Thevis were only 20 miles away. None of the other known killers were ever considered or investigated in the King-Hartsfield case.

In the newspapers, authorities said the victims were shot with a double-barrel shotgun. *How did they know that? They didn't know it. There was no gun found at the scene. It was an assumption. In order to keep this from confusing you, I'll share a little information as to why they said it was a double-barrel shotgun. The GBI laboratory's findings were that the markings cut into the brass portion of the evidence shells were created when the shells were ejected from the gun, and these marking were unique to the break-top, single and double-barrel shotguns. It is my belief that they chose to go with the double-barrel that early in the investigation because it would have given the killer an advantage when killing two people.*

This double-barrel type gun could explain how the killer was able to get two rounds off very fast, one after the other in order to bring down two victims so close together who fell almost side by side. **See Figure 4: Stephens Arms break-top shotgun.** *Jerry had only a single-shot shotgun.*

❖ ❖ ❖

The morning of November 8, 1974, the morning after the murders, two 12-gauge shotgun shell casings were found at the crime scene. The Georgia Crime Laboratory, operated by the GBI, released their findings that the two casings had been fired from Jerry Banks' shotgun.

On December 11th 1974, the news was all over town. The police had made an arrest in the double murder case of two Clayton County citizens, a high-school teacher and a student. The arrest was made by the Henry County Sheriff's Department. The arrest of their suspect, Jerry Banks, the black man who claimed he had found the bodies, came after the State Crime Lab results proved that Mr. Banks' gun had been used in the murders.

The Sheriff's Department reported that they had made an arrest of their suspect, and they found the murder weapon in his home. WOW, imagine that! They found the murder weapon in his home. They made it sound like maybe he was hiding it from them. Jerry Banks was standing there along-side of the road waiting for the police while holding his shotgun in his hand the night he reported the murders.

As if that wasn't enough, on December 13, 1974, Detective Phillip Howard ordered another search of the crime scene, and Officer Bill Hart found a third shell. The third shell was given to GBI at that time at the crime scene. It also was fired from Jerry's shotgun.

CHAPTER 6

Georgia v. Banks I

Jerry Banks was arrested on December 11, 1974. He was indicted by a grand jury of Henry County, Georgia on January 13, 1975. The day of the trial came quickly on January 27, 1975.

I can't help but notice how fast things happened in Henry County. I'm sure there was a good reason for it!

Oddly enough Jerry Bank's court-appointed lawyer was the caliber Jerry needed. This lawyer began his law practice in 1970. He was a young lawyer and I believe he would have done an outstanding job for Jerry at that time. I base this on what I know of that lawyer. His firm represents our family today.

But Jerry was black and this lawyer was white, and everybody else involved in this case was white.

The Banks family lived in Stockbridge, just north of McDonough, with roots spanning many generations. Martin Luther King Sr. (referred to as Daddy King by his family and friends) and his family were also originally from Stockbridge and I was told "they were family." It is said that the Banks family went to Atlanta to seek legal advice. In January of 1975, the court-appointed attorney was replaced with an African-American lawyer, Attorney Hudson John Myers, from Atlanta. Hudson John Myers was brought in to take over State v. Banks. I was told this was the biggest mistake ever made in regard to Jerry Banks' life.

A powerful statement made to me by one of Jerry Banks' many lawyers was, "Jerry Banks paid dearly for their ... involvement."

One reason why this statement was true: Jerry Banks was on trial for his life and the shell casings found at the scene were going to put him in the electric chair, and Attorney Hudson John Myers brought only two witnesses to court, Mrs. Grace Slaughter and Perry Banks.

⚜ ⚜ ⚜

This case against Jerry Banks came down to several points.

On January 29, 1975, Mrs. Slaughter took the stand, telling the jury Jerry Banks was at her house most of that day until 5:00 p.m. and there was no way he could have been in the area when the murders happened at 2:30 p.m. The jury foreman, John Chappell, said the time just didn't work out for Jerry to be at her house at 5:00 p.m. and at the crime scene at 5:00 p.m. in time to find the bodies as he said he did. Mrs. Slaughter got her time all wrong when she said 5:00 p.m.

Jerry had already stated that he had never hunted that area or dropped any shell casings in the area. There was Perry Banks' testimony that he had used that shotgun in that area but today, looking back, Perry Banks doesn't even remember his testimony and when asked if it were true. ... "Probably not," he said. But anything Perry or Mrs. Slaughter would have said that day would not have helped.

The jury was told how Jerry Banks was found at the scene of the crime with a shotgun under his arm by himself.

And then there was Mr. King's wallet. It was the testimony of Sgt. Tommy Floyd that Jerry had stated in one story that he picked up the wallet from the area of the pools of blood and another story of how he removed it from Marvin King's pocket. When you give conflicting statements to the police, you are considered lying and therefore a prime suspect.

Sgt. Tommy Floyd testified the Crime Lab report showed the shells found at the crime scene came from Jerry's shotgun. In the minds of the jury, the shells found at the scene were too much evidence against the defendant.

Being there was no testimony from a so-called motorist saying Jerry freely flagged him down asking him to call for help; it appeared to the jury that Jerry Banks was alone. It was stated that Jerry made up the story of the motorist and his story to bolster Jerry's own story. That's right! The motorist was a no-show at the trial. Attorney Hudson John Myers ran an ad in the newspaper before the first trial, seeking any information about the mystery motorist, but no reply ever came.

⟡ ⟡ ⟡

Attorney Hudson John Myers did argue, and with the help of the State's witness, Kelly Fite, from the Crime lab, that there was no proof the pellets found in the victims came from the precise shells found at the scene nor that the pellets were fired from Jerry's shotgun.

The one thing the state could never show was motive. On the stand and in a statement to the newspaper, Sgt. Tommy Floyd stated that he was not comfortable with any motive on Jerry's part. Sgt. Floyd stated in court that, before the trial, he took a trip to see Perry Banks. He explained, he had asked Perry Banks if he could think of any reason why Jerry would have committed such a brutal murder. Perry Banks said "No". Tommy Floyd knew of Jerry, Perry, and Hardrock. Without a clear motive, Sgt. Tommy Floyd was not comfortable accepting the case. He felt there was more to the story than what was being told.

Staying with the motive thought here a bit longer: how many times in your life have you read the headlines, "Thirty-eight-year-old male teacher found murdered with a 19-year-old former female student in the woods at 2:30 p.m. on a school day?" Oh, and in another county.

I don't mean to speak for everyone here, but I guess we are supposed to believe it when they say a young black hunter robbed and killed them. Motive should account for something.

Okay, a robbery at 2:30 p.m. on a Saturday, I could buy that. But these victims were supposed to be at work at that time of day on a Thursday. The bigger question here, before you ever get to who killed them, is what in the world were they doing there in the first place? And was this normal for them?

Once you resolve that, then you ask was Jerry Banks connected to their being on Rock Quarry Road? Melanie's 1965 Ford was found five miles away at the intersection of highway 138 and 42 in Stockbridge in the opposite direction from Jonesboro. **See Figure 8: Routes Taken by Miss Hartsfield and Mr. King**. Was Jerry Banks connected to that? These two people did not have time to drive all the way to Henry County that day and return to their jobs in Clayton County, even if all they did were drive through without stopping and then return. These two victims were supposed to be at work by 12 noon. They were not murdered until 2:30 p.m.

Is it possible that Jerry Banks killed over what little money Marvin King had or didn't have in his wallet? If Jerry Banks' motive had been theft, why were their rings and watches not taken? Why was Marvin King's gun not taken? I will bet any amount of money an FBI profiler would agree this was a murder of anger and revenge by someone who not only knew the victims but had some kind of dealings. It was personal. Jerry Banks just didn't fit the profile.

When considering motive, it seems logical to also take into consideration the profile of a suspect. I have given much thought over the years as to the type of person who could shoot two people twice, once in the back and again in the back of the head with a shotgun at very close range.

These were not robbers. They were paying someone back or sealing their lips. The first two shots would have to be within a few seconds of each other. To me, this individual would be no different than an al-Qaeda member cutting off the heads of Americans. This kind of person feels nothing at all and no remorse. This would not have been his first kill. This crime was committed with no hesitation and with the skills of a pro, yet with the carelessness of one who is working in his protected turf and with no fear of getting caught. This was not the work of one person, surely not a person like Jerry Banks. There were actions taken to impede the finding of the bodies, not to facilitate it.

You will learn later, there were actions taken to insure the victims would cross over the Henry County line that morning. This was a premeditated and a well-planned assault by at least two or more people. I could go on all day about the mind-set of a person who was this callous. This was no robbery.

❖ ❖ ❖

This case was a total mystery from the very beginning because basically there was no concrete evidence found anywhere at anytime that pointed toward Jerry Banks, other than those evidence shells found at the crime scene. There wasn't much need for anything else. Even a signed confession from anyone else would not have helped Jerry Banks. The victims were white and the Henry County Sheriff's Department and the District Attorney said Banks murdered those people for their money.

District Attorney Ed McGarity stood before the jury and stated Jerry Banks had, in the past, served a year and seven months for involuntary manslaughter for accidently shooting a man.

"This man has no regard for human life. He took 3 lives. Why shouldn't he give his own?"

It was my lack of understanding that led me to believe that the people of Henry County as a whole were in agreement with the court, that they had their man and that these people had been inconvenienced long enough. But that was far from the truth. I have questioned hundreds of people from Henry County, white and black, and not one person knew what really happened in this case, and not one person felt Jerry Banks was guilty. Well to tell the truth retired Detective Paul Robbins did say Jerry Banks got what he deserved.

❖ ❖ ❖

The trial lasted every bit of 1½ days of testimony. After a day of deliberations with no decision, Judge Hugh Sosebee sequestered the jury, keeping them in a local McDonough motel that night. By noon the next day the jury had come to a verdict.

The Atlanta paper said Virginia had been allowed to be at Jerry's side at the defendant's table during the trial, but during the reading of the verdict and penalty, she was placed with the spectators by orders from Judge Sosebee. She sat with Perry and when the verdict was read, Perry and Virginia Banks were overcome with emotion and tears welled in their eyes.

Jerry had sat next to Attorney Hudson John Myers the entire trial and never said a word and then, as he heard "Your honor, we find the defendant guilty on two counts of murder," he again sat there like an obedient slave and took his beating.

To me, it was a lot like in the movie Glory, when the black soldier, played by Denzel Washington, took his beating. At first, as the cat of nine tails cut into his back, his face revealed no expression. He was not going to give that power to the white man. However, near the end, no matter how hard the young man tried to hold back the tears and his outward emotions, they surfaced and showed the world his heart.

Jerry Banks was not there yet. He was not ready to let these white people see a broken man. Jerry thought in the beginning they would see he didn't kill anybody. He was wrong. As he sat there, he knew what was going on, but there wasn't anything he could do, other than pray. He wasn't the first black man to go through something like this. I'm sure he did sit there in court and most defiantly took it like a man.

They say Jerry's mother was with his three small children across the street just outside of the court house playing in the town square under the 100-year-old oak trees. Their lives as well would never be the same.

After four more hours, the jury of seven men and five women returned their decision as to the sentencing phase. Jerry Banks would be put to death in the electric chair between the hours of 10:00 a.m. and 4:00 p.m. on January 16, 1976, in Reidsville State Prison in South Georgia.

Other than the three shell casings, the only other piece of evidence found at the crime scene was the shoe prints, but they were never talked about in court. I'm not sure why that information was omitted. Were they Jerry's prints? Not one statement was ever raised to show the prints were or were not from Jerry Banks' boots.

PART II:

ANOTHER DOG AND PONY SHOW

CHAPTER 7

The Bullpen

Jerry Banks was born on January 18th, 1951, and he had spent his 24th birthday in the bullpen. Now he was going to die before his 25th birthday for something he didn't do. This was not the way Jerry Banks planned his life to work out.

After the trial Jerry found himself back in the jail house, better known as the "bullpen" in McDonough, waiting to be transferred to Reidsville State Prison. The bullpen was a little brick building that couldn't have been more than 50 foot by 50 foot. The courthouse faced South and the jail sat on the East side of the courthouse facing East on Lawrenceville Street. It didn't matter if you were held for a double-parking violation or a double-murder conviction. You were all thrown in together.

I recently stopped by and visited the bullpen, which now serves as a center for helping troubled juveniles. I introduced myself to the manager and gave a little background about Jerry and the building's history. He was a newcomer from up North, a black man himself, who was moved by my quick synopsis, and he allowed me to spend some time where Jerry Banks was held for so long.

The bars are still there on the windows, keeping people out these days. I was drawn to the old steel door and found myself slowly moving my open hand over the initials left behind by the prisoners in hopes of finding Jerry's. I knew they were there somewhere under one of those old coats of gray paint. My journey and Jerry's nightmare again intersected.

Just outside the towering, burly back door, off to one side was where the old trailer sat many years ago. They used it as the Sheriff's Office. The back door was a large steel door that looked like something from Fort Knox. This was the door used to move prisoners to and from the courthouse. This door is still covered with decades and decades of prisoner's initials.

✣ ✣ ✣

It was on February 4, 1975, four days after Jerry Banks was sentenced to die, when Mr. Andrew Lake Eberhardt, the missing motorist, came forward and announced his shocking story to Judge Hugh Sosebee and told him that Jerry flagged him down the day of the murders. He explained that he did not appear at the trial because he was never called. Judge Sosebee made a few phone calls. When Attorney Hudson John Myers filed a motion with Judge Sosebee for a new trial, he was turned down. However, it was the failure to report this witness's name and statement to the defense by Sheriff Jimmy Glass that brought this case to the Georgia Supreme Court.

BY THE GEORGIA SUPREME COURT:

Arthur K. Bolton, Attorney General: FOR THE STATE

Hudson John Myers: FOR THE DEFENSE

"One of the appellant's grounds in his motion for a new trial was based on newly discovered evidence in that the identity of the passing motorist who was flagged down by the appellant was not discovered until after the trial. The state (The District Attorney Ed McGarity) contended, and the trial court (Judge Hugh Sosebee) agreed, that the testimony of Mr. Eberhardt, the passing motorist who called the police at the request of the appellant, would be merely cumulative of evidence produced at the trial. We do not agree with this conclusion and it is our opinion that the trial court erred, in not granting the appellant's motion, for a new trial on this ground."

On September 15th 1975, the ruling came down from the higher court ordering a new trial.

Now with the new trial, Jerry's hopes were high and his faith in God was stronger than ever. He wasn't going to allow these people to send him to death row for something he didn't do. Attorney Hudson John Myers returned to the bullpen with news that District Attorney Ed McGarity offered Jerry Banks a life sentence in exchange for a guilty plea. I guess the idea of Jerry sitting in prison for life and the District Attorney not having to go to trial again sat well with their office but Jerry said "No deal." He didn't kill those people and he wasn't going stand up there and say he did, even if it would save him from the electric chair.

CHAPTER 8

A Bond Between Two Strangers

Jerry's mother was married twice. Ludie Banks Jr. was her husband, who died around 1945, and he was Ludie Banks III's (Jerry's older half brother) father. Mrs. Banks had Jerry and then Perry with a second husband who passed away, but she gave them the Banks' name for her own reasons.

Jerry attended Smith Barnes in Stockbridge, a segregated school. He and his girl friend, Virginia Lemon, were sweethearts. I asked Perry if Jerry was a good-looking young man. He told me with a little laugh in his voice, "Yes. He was. All the girls loved him. He was light skinned with freckles, 5 foot 11 inches and weighed about 165 pounds."

The couple dropped out of school at the same time because their baby boy, Jerry Jr., was due to be born, followed by another son and a daughter.

Jerry was not afraid of work. I was told he worked at Riverdale Paving and the two of them lived in one of two small framed houses on Banks Rd, which ran off Rock Quarry Road between Highway 42 and Interstate 75 south of Atlanta. The Lemon family owned both houses and Virginia's aunt lived in the bigger of the two.

Perry Banks said they were raised in the church by their mother and that Jerry attended regularly, but as he got older he pulled away.

Being black in the South was difficult. But Jerry's grandfather, who died around 1997, had taught his family not to cross any white people, especially those in power. "They use to hang people in my day." He had come up in a time when they were hung for little or nothing.

I am not the first writer to write about Jerry Banks. <u>In Spite of Innocence: Erroneous Convictions in Capital Cases</u> by Michael L. Radelet, Hugo Adam Bedau, and Constance E. Putnam put together a collection of wrongful death convictions around the country. However, that type of book did not allow the writers to go beyond the fact that Jerry Banks was wrongfully convicted. These writers did point out Jerry Banks' previous manslaughter charge, but with no detail, much like District Attorney Ed McGarity informing the jury of this charge without any explanation.

According to Perry Banks, the truth about that case was this: Jerry was at a family get-together with his three brothers and their relatives who were raised on hunting and fishing, not robbing and killing people. Jerry's uncle had helped raise all the Banks boys and the area they lived in was as country, as you could get.

At this outdoor cook-out there was another cousin, Robert Lee Walker, who arrived late, who had borrowed Jerry's handgun earlier and handed it over at that time. Jerry placed the gun in his back pocket.

There was a bit of uneasiness in the air over Robert Lee Walker's presence because he had been borrowing something else, something from Ludie Banks ... Ludie's wife. The two men began arguing over this issue, and the conflict spread to all party members. Sides were taken. Robert Lee pulled a knife on Ludie and things quickly got out of control with all the tempers and alcohol. Jerry was trying to protect his family. He pleaded with his cousin to put down the knife. Jerry at some point pulled the gun out. Jerry tried reminding him over and over that they were all family. The anger was now to the point that Walker lunged at Ludie but Jerry put himself between his cousin and his brother. Jerry shot his cousin in the scuffle. He was arrested and was sent to the Henry County jail. Jerry's brother put his wife in the street and raised their children himself. The wheels of justice moved slowly for blacks, if at all. When investigators returned to the scene, over a year and seven months later, they discovered an old rusty knife in the weeds still lying there. Jerry Banks was freed.

I have had the pleasure of speaking with many people over the years from time to time who were around during those days and knew Jerry. In a conversation with Officer Charles Tomlinson he told me how he first met Jerry Banks. Detective Tomlinson, under Sheriff Cook, had become close with Jerry when he was in the bullpen for shooting his cousin in self-defense. Retired Detective Charles Tomlinson remembered Jerry's manslaughter conviction and he told me, he remembered the charges were dropped. It was during the year and seven months that Jerry spent in jail that Detective Tomlinson honestly got to know Jerry Banks. Jerry was a trustee during this unpleasant stay and Jerry made the best of it. After all, Jerry had killed his own cousin. Even though it was self-defense, it didn't make Jerry feel any better. Also during this time Tomlinson took Jerry from the jail one day and they attended a family member's funeral.

Charles Tomlinson told me, "I never felt like Jerry was guilty of the Quarry Road murders and felt like there was no way Jerry could have killed them, especially with that old shotgun." And he said, "Jerry was a fine young man that was not capable of murder."

❖ ❖ ❖

If there are times you think you hear my anger in my words, it's because I truly see and feel the pain of the downtrodden. In the 50's, it was the old black man carrying his worldly possessions in a brown Piggy Wiggly grocery bag, riding in the back of the bus behind the white line or the poor black children sitting on the front porch of their old shanties on a make-shift sofa, usually a back seat of an old automobile, along the old dusty Georgia roads. Even in the 1970s I would see the blacks having to order food through a small window at the sidewalk because they were thought to be not clean enough to enter a restaurant in the town of Metter, Georgia.

I may have given the impression that Mr. Banks and I were friends. I was once told by an editor from New Jersey who I worked with briefly that if I claim that to be true, even though we never met, "this would make you appear to be unstable and weak in the eyes of your readers." I have spoken of how I feel sadness in my heart every time I think of Jerry Banks, his wife and their children and what these people did to them. Compassion does not come through a handshake. Don't tell anyone, but I have never met Jesus Christ either.

I am not trying to come off as some kind of white Do-Good-er Crusader for the whole black population and their cause. It's just that all my life I have had a soft spot in my heart for poor people, people who have been mistreated or people who looked sad or down and out of luck. I don't care if they are white or black.

I was raised by my mother in middle Georgia during the 1950s to use the term "Colored" or "Negro." To this day I don't feel comfortable using the term "Black" in the presence of black people. I don't care what the government wants me to call anybody. I don't care for the term Afro or African-American. I have never in my life ever heard of an Afro-Canadian. If you are a citizen of the United States, you are an American.

My mother never in her life used any other term. It was my mother who taught me early about the injustice of the black people. Now I can't say I'm perfect. We all have bad days. I do however worship on Sunday with many blacks. I will say they make up about 30% of our members. You are either a good person or not. I don't choose my friends by the color of their skin and I believe a stranger is a friend that you haven't met yet.

To the people around here, in those days, a good motive would have been to point toward a black man and claim over a hundred and fifty years of hatred of white people. To expect them to accept that as a motive was normal. Why did their investigation bring them back to Jerry Banks? Was there something about this young man that could bring him to execute two human beings, like two rabid dogs? I don't think he would be considered the first black to do something like that. I mean blacks have killed whites and vise versa in the past with little or no motive other than just plain and simple payback.

If I were on a jury and told of Jerry Banks' motive for killing, I would accept it if it could be proven. However, I would need his motive for standing around for two and a half hours waiting for the police to arrive before I would accept his guilt. Motive is exactly that and nothing else, motive. To me, there is more than a fine line between motive and a reason to kill, and Jerry Banks had neither.

CHAPTER 9

Georgia v. Banks II

The date was November 17, 1975. The District Attorney Edward E. McGarity and Assistant District Attorney Mr. Harold Craig brought forth six of the Henry County Sheriff's Officers and three officials from the Georgia Bureau of Investigation as witnesses for the state.

The Defense Attorney Hudson John Myers again brought only two witnesses, Andrew Lake Eberhardt and Sheriff Jimmy Glass.

The subject matter, testimony and physical evidence in both trials were the same with the exception of the two witnesses called by the Defense in the first trial. Andrew Lake Eberhardt and Sheriff Jimmy Glass were called in place of Mrs. Grace Slaughter and Perry Banks, the introduction of the red bedspread and the fact that Lead Detective Phillip Howard was no longer employed by the Henry County Sheriff's Department were the only differences. This time I will examine in more detail the facts of the case. All testimony is from the proceedings, errors and all. *My comments are in italics.*

State of Georgia	**HENRY SUPERIOR CO**
Vs.	CASE #10032
Jerry Banks	**CHARGE: MURDER**

C.R. (Dick) Barnes, First having been duly sworn, testified as follows:

BY MR. MYERS:

After many questions and viewing the crime scene photos:
Q. And you received a call at 5:45 p.m. that evening?
A. That's correct.
Q. Now at the time you received that call, did the caller identify himself to you?
A. He at first stated his name. I did not catch his name or anything.
Q. Do you recall what the caller told you?
A. Yes, sir. He stated he was on his way home from work and he was coming down Rock Quarry Road; he was flagged down by a young black male with a shotgun, and he said he had been down there hunting and found two bodies in the woods and asked him to call the police. And also, he said he would be standing by the road until we arrived.

Moving forward in the trial, to now Lt. Tommy Floyd's statement, compare their testimony:

BY MR. MYERS:

Q. Lieutenant Floyd. Do you recall who notified you?
A. I intercepted the message; it wasn't really directed to me particularly at the time and I was nearby and responded to the call.
Q. What do you mean when you said intercepted the message?
A. I believe the dispatcher was giving the call to Detective Barnes and there was traffic back and forth, or conversations on the radio back and forth between the dispatcher and Detective Barnes about something to the effect of two bodies. ...

I have mentioned there are Sins of Henry County. Here is one example. The press, a jury, a judge and even the D.A. sat in court for two days and did not pick up on the differences in testimony during a death penalty trial and not one person acted on it, not one! Officer Barnes never talked to Andrew Eberhardt on the phone. Barnes led the court to think that, but he talked to the dispatcher, to whom Eberhardt gave his name and statement and his personal information.

Sgt. Tommy Floyd would not have heard any of Barnes's testimony because a witness is not allowed in the courtroom beforehand. I could see where the last person Sheriff Jimmy Glass wanted in the courtroom was the dispatcher.

The reason: The dispatcher wasn't in the loop, wouldn't lie under oath and more than likely the police log would show a record of Andrew Lake Eberhardt's phone call and his personal information.

You see, Andrew Lake Eberhardt was the witness Sheriff Jimmy Glass failed to remember and failed to report his name and statement to the defense. This omission brought this case to the Georgia Supreme Court after the 1st trial.

Without the dispatcher present during the first trial, Detective Barnes and Sheriff Glass could easily say they didn't remember the motorist's name and imply they could not contact him. Therefore, Andrew Lake Eberhardt was not present to help Jerry Banks.

Now I have been advised by counsel that Sheriff Jimmy Glass was under no obligation to provide any such information to anyone, unless asked. Does this mean there were no wrongs committed by Detective Barnes or Sheriff Glass? But what if testimony shows he was asked?

RETURNING TO DETECTIVE DICK BARNES' TESTIMONY:

BY MR. MYERS:

A. ... and also, he said he would be standing by the road until we arrived.
Q. Standing on the side of the road?"
A. Yes, sir.

The Defense Attorney Myers apparently found this extremely odd, and asked the officer if he found it was unusual for a call to come in like that.

Q. A caller, stating a black man who said he was hunting and found two bodies and asked him to call the police. And he told him to tell the police that I'll be standing by the road, waiting. That's what he said?

A. Yes, sir.

Now I don't know how killers normally work but I would guess that if you had just blown two people's brains all over the place, you would not stand alongside the road waiting for the police, with a shotgun in your hand, particularly if you were black.

By Mr. Myers:

Q. AT THE TIME YOU SAW BANKS STANDING ALONGSIDE THE ROAD, WHAT DID HE HAVE ON?

A. He was dressed in typical hunting clothes; an army field jacket, blue jeans and I believe, I'm not sure, a pair of army combat boots, and some sort of knit cap, stocking-type cap."

Q. You described that as being typical hunting attire?

A. Yes.

Defense Attorney Myers asked Officer Barnes if he ever checked Jerry Banks' shotgun to see if it had been fired.

Q. As a matter of fact, you didn't do anything with regard to this weapon at all?

A. No sir.

Q. Did you look inside to see if there were any spent rounds in the chamber at all?

A. No.

They didn't even know if Jerry's gun had been fired at all that day and they wanted to put him in the electric chair.

✥ ✥ ✥

By the time of the second trial Sgt. Floyd was now Lieutenant Floyd.

T. K. FLOYD, First having been duly sworn, testified as following:

DIRECT EXAMINATION BY (PROSECUTOR) MR. CRAIG:

Q. State your name, please.
A. Tommy Floyd.
Q. I show you what's marked State's Exhibit #1 and ask you if you can identify that, please.
A. Yes, sir. This is a single-barrel 12-gauge shotgun with black electrical tape over the fore piece which Jerry Banks had with him at the scene.
Q. Did you while you were there (at the scene) recover any other items of physical evidence that you took in ... in your investigation that you recall?
A. I believe around the bloodstains there was some wadding, some hair, pieces of what we believed to be skull and I believe that was all at that time.

FURTHER DIRECT EXAMINTION BY MR. CRAIG:

Q. Lieutenant Floyd, I believe when you were on the stand earlier, you said that on the 5th day of December, 1974, you and Detective Robbins went to the residence of Jerry Banks here in Henry County, Georgia, is that correct?
A. Yes, sir, that's correct.
Q. What was the purpose?
A. To talk with Jerry Banks and to borrow his shotgun for further tests. On December 4th, 1974, I received a call from Kelly Fite who identified Jerry's shotgun as the murder weapon. On the 5th, we talked with Jerry Banks; read him his rights; I asked him if we could borrow his shotgun again so we could take it to the Crime Lab.
Q. All right, did you have any occasion on any date after December 5th to question Jerry Banks either about the ... or anything else having to do with the murders?
A. Yes, sir, we did.

Q. What was the first occasion after December 5th?
A. On December 11th, an arrest warrant was issued for Jerry Banks. Detective Robbins and myself, executed this warrant and arrested Jerry Banks. The weapon that we received from Jerry Banks (on the 5th) had been taken to the Crime Lab. Upon receiving their report I then went to the Justice of the Peace Johnny Bond and asked that an arrest warrant be issued for Jerry Banks.

BY MR. MYERS:

Again we are in the second trial during November 17 and 18, 1975.
Q. Now, Captain Howard doesn't work for the Sheriff's Department anymore, does he? When did he leave?
A. The latter part of January 1975.
Q. Why did you not actively investigate the case after the (first) trial?
A. I felt like there had been a conclusion reached in the investigation.
Q. Now after the arraignment (January 9, 1975) you continued your investigating of the case?
A. Yes, sir.
Q. And do you recall what you told me at that time?
A. I told you that a specific motive for the two killings had not been uncovered or discovered or whatever.
Q. Now, we're in the second trial; have you been able to.... well, you haven't actively investigated since the first trial, so I guess that would answer the question and I won't even ask it. Let me ask you this question, Lieutenant Floyd, that is, did you as a result of your viewing the bodies at the crime scene on November 7th, 1974, were you able to determine that anyone had been bound, tied, gagged or whatever; was there any evidence of such when you arrived?
A. No, sir. ...
Q. Did you become the investigating officer at that time when you arrived on the scene or when did that designation ... when was that designation made?

A. I believe it was made some time during the day of November 8th. I wasn't ... Captain (Phillip) Howard was in command of the case on November 7th, during the crime scene.

Q. And you were placed in charge of the investigation some time during November 8th?

A. Yes, Sir. Well, Captain Howard was overseeing the investigation, he was in charge, but he directed me to be in charge of the field investigation itself.

Q. Now, while you were in charge of field investigation, did you rope the crime scene at all?

A. No, Sir, I didn't. Like I say, I wasn't in charge of the crime scene at all.

Q. Not at all ... What do you mean by field investigation?

A. Well, interviewing witnesses, prospective witnesses, following leads, what have you.

In the above questions of Lieutenant Floyd by Defense Attorney Hudson John Myers, he asked one question that he asked many times during the second trial, "When did Lead Detective Phillip Howard leave the Sheriff's Department?" It was always answered the same.

Attorney Myers never pushed this issue beyond this point. It seems to me that he wanted the jury to hear over and over that Detective Phillip S. Howard left the department at the end of January, 1975. Why, was that date so important? I'll tell you why. The latter part of January 1975 would have been during the middle of Jerry Banks' first trial. Jerry Banks was ordered to die in the electric chair in Reedsville State Prison on January 31, 1975. Lead Detective Phillip Howard had to have been released before or during the trial. When asked if his leaving the department had anything to do with the way this case was handled, the prosecution objected.

✥ ✥ ✥

One of the first procedures in the original investigation and in this trial was the autopsies of the two victims. This was performed by a Dr. Howard from the State Crime Lab (not to be confused with Detective Phillip

Howard.) He testified he was called at approximately 7:15 p.m. the day of the murders and arrived at the coroner's near 11:00 p.m.

Dr. Howard of the GBI: First having been duly sworn, testified as follows:

DIRECT EXAMINATION BY MR. McGARITY:

Q. Now Dr. Howard, where did you get your education?
A. I have a Bachelor's Degree in Chemistry and Bacteriology from the University of Montana; have a Doctor's Degree from the graduate portion of Medical School, University of Minnesota: did post-doctorate work in pathology at Emory University and under Dr. Herman Jones, the former Director of the Georgia Laboratory.
Q. Why were you in Henry County, Georgia, on November 7, 1974?
A. I responded to a call from the coroner, from Coroner Ronnie Stewart, at approximately 7:15 p.m. and came to Carmichael's Funeral Home here in McDonough.
Q. Were these two people identified to you as Marvin King and Melanie Ann Hartsfield?
A. Yes, sir, they were. Miss Hartsfield was identified at the Funeral Home by Don Mason and C.H. McPherson and Marvin King was identified to me by C.H. McPherson Sr., also at the Funeral Home.
(After many photos)
Q. All right, now Doctor, I ask you if you did an autopsy on Marvin King?
A. Yes, sir, I did.
Q. Will you tell us what you found?
A. * The body showed the presence of two shotgun wounds; one shotgun wound entered the left [sic] elbow ... entered the upper arm just above the left [sic] elbow, measured approximately one and a half inches in diameter, passed through the elbow and re-entered the left [sic] side, passed in back of the main body cavity, sectioned the spinal column and spinal cord in the lower back area. And one shot

exited from the right [*sic*] side of his spinal column approximately four inches to the right [*sic*] side of the spinal column. Shots were recovered from the path of the charge and were identified as 00 Buckshot. The right [*sic*] arm near the entry also showed a wadding contusion and abrasion; that is, a bruise from the charge. Mr. King also had a shotgun wound of entry in the back of the head, almost in the center of the head (the base of the skull) which exited ... and this charge exited from just to the left side of the midline in the forehead. The body also showed extensive drag marks, that is, on the arm and on the front of the body where his body had been dragged and abraded from the passage of the body over a rough surface and these abrasion marks were over the ribs and chest area, on the right cheek, and the blood from this subject was checked for alcohol with negative results.

* (*Note this is an error [either by lack of memory from the first trial or a transcription error]. The gunshot entered King's right elbow and right side.*)

Dr. Howard started performing these autopsies at 11:00 p.m. that night and determined that the time of death was around 2:30 p.m., about eight hours earlier on that day.

Q. Now, Dr. Howard, did you make an autopsy of Melanie Ann Hartsfield?

A. Yes, major evidence of injury were two shotgun wounds, one of which was in the right side of the neck and exited through the top of her head ... there were no shot or wadding along the track although there was some carbon staining and some tattoo marks at the neck indicating the muzzle-to-target distance was not extremely long. There was another shotgun wound of entry in the left side of the back which passed through the abdominal aorta and there were at least three associated pellet marks of exit in the abdominal area, so the entrance wound in the left side of the back with three large pellets exiting from the right front. The charge lacerated the liver and sectioned the abdominal aorta. Either one of these wounds would have been fatal. This body also had drag marks that included the breast and chest area indicated, and extended from bottom to top indicating she had been dragged on her stomach feet first over a considerable distance.

Q. I present to you State's Exhibit #26 and ask you if you can identify that?

A. This is wadding and shot removed from the abdominal cavity of Melanie Ann Hartsfield.

Q. What did you do with that?

A. I took that back to the Laboratory and turned it over to Mr. Fite.

Q. Now, do you have an opinion, Doctor, as to which shot was fired first on both bodies? In other words, were both bodies shot in the back?

A. One body was shot in the back and one body was ... well, yes, both bodies were shot in the back. Both bodies were shot in the head and both were also shot in the trunk area.

Q. Now, based on your examination of shotgun wounds. Let's assume a person was on the ground face down and a person was standing away from them five or ten feet with a shotgun and the trigger was pulled and the discharge of the shotgun entered the base of the neck or head of the female victim, what angle would it protrude from?

A. The wound from the head of the male victim extends through at about a forty-five-degree angle. The wound through the head of the female victim makes about a thirty-degree angle with her vertical axis; in other words, if she is horizontal on the ground, the wound would travel through at about thirty degrees from the vertical axis of the body.

Q. Then, Doctor, would you say or could you say that these people, King and Hartsfield, had been shot from the back first and then shot later while they were on the ground?

A. It would be my opinion that they were both shot in the trunk to start with while they were standing erect and then they were both shot in the head after they had fallen.

BY THE COURT:

Q. Do you have an opinion, Dr. Howard as to how far the muzzle of the barrel would have been from either one of these wounds you referred to?
A. Well, it varies some, Judge. I doubt if the maximum distance of the wounds would have been more than ten feet and a minimum distance less than three feet.

BY MR. McGARITY:

Q. Doctor, how many autopsies have you completed in the State of Georgia?
A. Approximately 4,000.
Q. And during this time that you made these autopsies on people that have been reported to you, allegedly killed by someone, what type of killing would you say this was?
A. I'm not sure that I understand your question. Certainly the wound in the head are what we typically see as coup de grace wounds; make sure the victim is dead, but other than that, I'm not sure what you're referring to.
Q. Now, Doctor during this examination, I ask you whether or not that you made a pelvic examination of Melanie Ann Hartsfield?
A. I did, yes, sir.
Q. What ... was your findings?
A. Negative ... the vagina was dry.
Q. All right, I ask you the same question; did you examine the male organs of Marvin King?
A. Yes, sir.
Q. And what ...were the results of that examination?
A. I found no evidence of recent sexual intercourse.

BY MR. McGARITY: ALL RIGHT, HE IS WITH YOU.

CROSS EXAMINATION BY MR. MYERS:

Q. Dr. Howard, was Dr. Foster with you?
A. You bet.
Q. Is Dr. Foster an MD.
A. Yes, sir.
Q. Are you?
A. No, sir.
Q. What ... is the differences?
A. Well, in this particular case, he practices medicine as well as Medical Examiner. In my case, I don't practice medicine; I examine dead bodies. I have a PHD from Medical School. He has a MD from Medical School.
Q. All right, you and Dr. Foster. Okay, now what is the purpose of an autopsy?
A. To determine the cause, manner and circumstances of death.
Q. Cause, manner and circumstances of death.
A. Yes, sir.
Q. That's all that an autopsy can do?
A. I think that covers a pretty broad field.
Q. Cause, manner and circumstances?
A. Yes, sir.
Q. That's what your testimony has been about?
A. Yes, sir.
Q. What is the cause of death?
A. Cause of death; shotgun wounds to the bodies.
Q. Now, do you know how many different kinds of shotguns there are?
A. Well, if you mean by kinds, I think you have to guess because they are made anywhere from legitimate gun shops to private collectors to little machine shops in Czechoslovakia.
Q. In other words, the question I'm asking; in determining cause, you do not also identify weapon?
A. I identify it as a shotgun, and 12-gauge and the type of ammunition, but I don't identify make, no, sir.

The "make" (the manufacturer) of ammunition, not the type or make of shotguns is the subject in question here. The type of shotgun these shells came from (12-gauge) had already been identified by Kelly Fite, the ballistic expert who will testify later.

> Q. All right ... you identify gauge?
> A. Yes, sir.
> Q. Now, how do you do that?
> A. Well, one thing you can do is count the number of pellets. Another thing you can do is to measure the size of the wadding.
> Q. Now, which did you do?
> A. Here it's very simple because (double ought) 00 buckshot is only found in 12-gauge shells to my recollection.
> Q. Oh, 00 buckshot is only found in 12-gauge?
> A. That's my recollection. And here we also have wadding which confirms 12-gauge, so there's no real problem.
> Q. Okay, so the basis of that is the fact that 00 buckshot only comes in 12-gauge?
> A. Now, wait a minute. I said that we have two criteria; the size of the wadding and the size number of buckshot, so I'm not limiting it to a single criterion and I don't recall testifying that it was a 12-gauge shotgun.
> Q. Well, I thought you said that a minute ago?
> A. I did not.
> Q. You did not?
> A. No. Oh, I said it to your query. Yes, it is a 12-gauge shotgun.

BY THE COURT:

> Q. What did you say, Dr. Howard as to what wadding and what shot?
> A. In direct testimony, I did not testify as to what size shotgun it was.

BY MR. MYERS:

> Q. That's what I wanted to know, I wanted to know if you had made a determination as to the type of shotgun.

BY THE COURT:

Q. When you say type, you mean gauge?

BY MR. MYERS: YES, SIR.

BY THE WITNESS:

A. I did not, but if you asked me, I would say it was a 12-gauge shotgun.
Q. You did not make a determination, but you will now?
A. I know it was a 12-gauge shotgun because of the size of the wadding and the size of the buckshot. ...
Q. Size of the wadding. ...
A. ...but I didn't make this determination myself; other people in the Crime Lab did; are you with me?
Q. Oh, you didn't make the determination independently?
A. No.
Q. Then I got to talk to people in the Crime Lab to see what their basis was?
A. They will be available.

BY THE COURT:

Q. Who is the ballistic person?
A. Kelly Fite.
That was, to me, the most damaging testimony against Lead Detective Phillip Howard and no one, other than Defense Attorney Hudson John Myers and Detective Phillip Howard, may have known it.
Doctor Howard had just testified that all he could determine from the wadding and pellets was that the ammunition used appeared to be a gauge of 12, making the murder weapon a 12-gauge shotgun. This would have been his observation the night of the autopsies, sometime between midnight and three or four in the morning. He did not know the make or manufacturer of the ammunition by the wadding or the pellets.

You will need to make note here of Dr. Howard's finding that he could only determine the gauge of the shell, not the manufacturer of the ammunition used in the murders. To me this was the most important factor in the entire murder case in determining who killed Marvin King and Melanie Ann Hartsfield.

⊕ ⊕ ⊕

Kelly Fite: First having been duly sworn, testified as following:

BY MR. MCGARITY:

Q. All right, would you remove that from the bag itself and hold it up. What did you do with the particular red sweater (which belonged to Melanie) that came out of State's Exhibit #14?

A. Well there is a gunshot hole of entry in the back of the sweater and this is what I paid special attention to.

Q. All right, what was the purpose of your examining that red sweater?

A. Well, it was to get an idea or to determine the muzzle-to-target distance or the distance from the end of the shotgun to the clothing and also, examination of this hole also indicated to me the type of ammunition used to make this hole.

Q. And how did it do that?

A. Well, in Winchester Western type buckshot, they pack the buckshot in polyethylene granules and this keeps the shot from banging against each other and deforming with the purpose of making the shot firing more accurate. I noticed there are numerous particles of this, polyethylene granules, on the ... around the entry hole in the back of the sweater.

Q. The polyethylene particles that, you found in the sweater, are they peculiar to Winchester Western shells ... are they unique or does any other manufacturer use that same type packing?

A. Well, they are unique to Winchester Western type buckshot.

Keep in mind it was Kelly Fite who determined the manufacturer of the ammunition and that would have been on November 8, 1974, which would have been on Friday.

BY THE COURT:

Q. Mr. Fite, did you have an occasion to form an opinion as to the distance of the muzzle of the gun from the sweater that you examined?

A. Yes, sir, I did, I fired test patterns with State's Exhibit #1, the 12-gauge shotgun, and compared these tests with Winchester Western 00 buckshot and compared my test with holes shown in this sweater and I came to the conclusion that the muzzle-to-target distance was approximately five feet.

✥ ✥ ✥

During this second trial, Sheriff Jimmy Glass was asked "Who were the investigating officers?" He named all the Officers: Lead Detective Phillip Howard, Tommy Floyd, Bill Hart, Billy Payne, Paul Robbins and Dick Barnes, Ted Ray, then he added Charles Tomlinson and Johnny Glover and I believe he mentioned Detective Bobby Lemon. These last three were black.

Could that be an outright lie? Did he want it to appear there were black and white officers involved in the investigation? Could that have been a simple mistake?

Two of these men were kept totally out of the investigation. Charles Tomlinson was a Sgt. then later Glass made him a Detective. But he told me he was never involved in this case and Johnny Glover was a Deputy on the force, not an investigator. Sgt. Johnny Glover confirmed to me he never was a part of the investigation.

Again according to records, Sgt. Johnny Glover was the officer who found Marvin King's vehicle during a routine patrol in the early morning hours the next morning after the killings. **See Figure 5: Aerial Photograph of Crime Scene**. Officer Charles Tomlinson was said to be with Detective Dick Barnes as they were the first to arrive at the murder scene. That was their only role.

✧ ✧ ✧

The television stations and the newspapers quoted no details made by Sheriff Jimmy Glass, Detectives Phillip S. Howard, Paul Robbins and Dick Barnes which would have raised a lot of eyebrows had they been heard outside of the courtroom. But "The truth and nothing but the truth, so help you God," was filled with lots of "mistakes" and also lies under oath. What is the statute of limitation for perjury? What is the statute of limitation for violating one's civil rights?

✧ ✧ ✧

There was nothing presented by Attorney Myers to make anybody change the minds of the jury. The second trial was a bigger joke than the first. Well, this time it did last two full days and Attorney Hudson John Myers called two new witnesses, Mr. Eberhardt and Sheriff Jimmy Glass. Attorney Myers got a second chance to prove Banks was innocent and all he could do was bring Mr. Eberhardt and Jimmy Glass into the courtroom to fight it out. About the only thing Mr. Eberhardt proved was he had met Sheriff Jimmy Glass at the scene of the crime and also informed the Sheriff he was going to be available for the trial, if they would just let him know when he would be needed. Sheriff Glass said he didn't recall anything about this man, either meeting him or talking to him on the phone before the first trial.

Attorney Myers brought no one to dispute the shotgun shell evidence or the improbabilities of Banks being able to fire an old single-barrel shotgun fast enough to commit the murders.

There was no defense to rebut the ballistics test. Those three shells again proved to the jury that Jerry Banks was guilty of two murders. That was good enough for the jury.

If I were on the jury hearing that evidence, the way it was presented and if I did not have the knowledge I have now, I would have found him guilty also. No! No I wouldn't ... anyone with any common sense should have been able to see it would have been impossible for Jerry to kill two people with that shotgun, plain and simple. If you do not share that belief at this time, that is okay. You have to consider I knew in 1974 Jerry Banks was innocent and that was a long time before I read the court records.

Throughout this trial there was more testimony about when things were done rather than what, why, and where. I'll give Attorney Myers a pat on the back for that. He didn't have a prayer in hell of winning this case even if he were given ten trials, with all things being equal. The first time I read the trial transcripts, I thought he was out of his mind and I still do, but he knew something was wrong. He knew there had to be a detective behind the wood pile. He knew the deck was stacked. The cards were not in Myers' favor. The jury was against Jerry Banks because they were told his gun was used to kill Marvin King and Melanie Ann Hartsfield and he was found at the crime scene with that gun. Those were the facts and that was all they needed.

⚜ ⚜ ⚜

PHILLIP STEWART HOWARD (Lead Detective): First having been duly sworn, testified as follows:

DIRECT EXAMINATION BY MR. MCGARITY:

- Q. Please state your name.
- A. Phillip Stewart Howard.
- Q. I'll ask you whether or not you had an occasion to be at the scene on the morning of the 8th of November?

A. Yes, I was.
Q. And do you recall, was there anyone with you?
A. Yes, sir there was Detective Ray.
Q. All right ... and I'll ask you whether or did ... that you found anything at the time?
A. Yes, sir I did.
Q. What did you find?
A. I found a Winchester shotgun casing. It was in the wooded area in the scene.
Q. And I'll ask you whether or not that you noticed any blood there at the scene?
A. Yes, sir I did.
Q. And I'll ask you whether or not that you can tell the Court and the Jury approximately how far from the blood spots there that this shell was?
A. Yes, sir, the shell that I found was approximately 37 feet from the bloodstain we believe belonged to Miss Hartsfield and 35 feet 4 inches from the bloodstain we believed was of Marvin King.
Q. I'll ask you if Mr. Ray found anything ... there?
A. Yes, sir, approximately ... I'd say five minutes or so after I discovered mine, he found one also of the same type.
Q. I present to you State's Exhibit #19 and ask you to examine it.
A. <u>They are Winchester Western XX Super X 00 Buck, Mark V shotgun casing, 12- gauge.</u>
Q. Now, after you received these shells marked State's Exhibit #19, what did you do with them?
A. I took these shells and they was [sic] brought back to my office and locked [sic] in my desk and they was in turn given to Detective Floyd and Detective Paul Robbins and they was [sic] carried to the Crime Lab.
Q. All right, sir, now Mr. Howard I present to you State's Exhibit #1 and ask you if you can identify it?
A. Yes, sir, that's a 12-gauge Stevens single shot shotgun, yes, sir.
Q. And I'll ask you did you do anything with the gun?
A. Yes, sir, I did. I instructed Detective Barnes to pick up the weapon and bring it to me in my office and <u>I took</u>

the weapon out into the yard and in front of the detective's trailer, right at the rear of the courthouse, and that was on November 10, and on November 10th, I fired that weapon three times.

Q. I present to you State's Exhibit #20 and ask you if you can identify them?

A. Yes, sir, I can. These are the three shells or three shotgun casings, 12-gauge; one Peters, one Remington and the other Remington, that I fired in the rear of the trailer marked with my handwriting and initials on the back.

Q. And do you know what happened to those?

A. They were also transported to the State Crime Lab For firing pin and pressure check.

Q. Who did you turn them over to, do you know?

A. Those were turned over to Floyd and Robbins, also.

BY MR.MCGARITY: He's with you.

BY MR. MYERS:

Q. Do you know of your knowledge what happened to Jerry Banks ... do you know how long Banks remained in the trailer that night?

A. No.

Q. Do you know whether he was under arrest at the time?

A. Did I ... He was there to give a statement, yes.

Q. Do you know which one of these shells you found?

A. No.

Q. But you found one of these?

A. Yes.

Q. What time were they found?

A. I'd say we got back to the scene around first light, I imagine anywhere from 7:30 to 9:00, I didn't make a time, exact time when they were found, no.

Q. And 45 minutes after you found yours, you said Detective Hart found his?

A. Four to five

Q. Four to five minutes.

A. Right.
Q. Detective Hart found his.
A. Detective Ray.
Q. I'm very sorry ... Detective Ray found the other shell?
A. Yes.
Q. Mr. Howard what date did you fire that weapon for the first time?
A. November 10, 1974, I fired three 12-gauge shells in the presence of C. R. Barnes.
Q. Into the ground?
A. There's a dirt pile right beside the chimney right down at the end of the courthouse, yes, and <u>I fired it into that from you might say the end of the trailer</u> down there.

Detective Phillip Howard said he fired the shotgun "<u>in front of the detective's trailer</u>", "<u>in the rear of the trailer</u>" and "<u>you might say the end of the trailer</u>". There are three different versions of where Lead Detective Phillip S. Howard testified he test fired Exhibit #1, all one right after the other. He could have been confused; someone could have been moving that dirt pile around. Don't jump to any conclusions yet, it only gets better.

Q. Now, you fired this, two days, after you found two shells on November 8th, 1974?
A. According to the reports, yes sir.
Q. Now, where were the two shells that you found on November 8th, where were they on November 10th when you fired the State's Exhibit #1?
A. On December 2nd, the three shells was [sic] fired from the Banks gun; they was [sic] carried by Detective Robbins to the Crime Lab and the two that we found on the scene; the two that you got stuck on your fingers.

Again he did not answer the question from Attorney Myers without a remark from Judge Sosebee.

Q. On November 10th, where were the two shells you found on November 8th, 1974?
A. Crime Lab.
Q. Well when did they go to the Crime Lab?

A. I believe they went there on the 8th.
Q. And these shells were fired by you on November 10th?
A. According to the report, yes sir.
Q. So you had the weapon in your possession then on November 10th?
A. Yes, sir I did.
Q. When did you get it?
A. <u>Detective Barnes picked that weapon up for me that morning.</u>

I think I like this next answer better than all of Detective Phillip Howard's answers combined.

Q. When did you first see the weapon on November 10th, was it in the morning or in the afternoon?
A. It must have been ... oh, I'd say it must have been ... whenever Detective Barnes brought it, into the office ... is the first time I saw it, that day, yes.

Was that an answer? Defense Attorney Hudson John Myers knew he had those guys on the hot seat. But without Jerry disputing their word, he could not go into these areas. If he had put Jerry Banks on the stand, I think he would have won that trial. You can tell when someone has something to hide. Remember what I said ... when they couldn't remember, they were lying; and when they were lying, you need to pay special attention to what they were "not remembering."

Let's compare these two answers of the witnesses. Go back one more question to Detective Phillip Howard's answer to Attorney Hudson Myers' question.

BY HUDSON MYERS: (QUESTION #1 TO DETECTIVE PHILLIP HOWARD)

Q. When did you get it (the gun)?
A. Detective Barnes picked that weapon up for me that morning.
He still did not answer the question.

Now looking back to when Officer Dick Barnes was asked the same question by Mr. Myers earlier, the same day.
Q. What did Captain Howard tell you to go there for; why did he tell you to go there?
A. He told me to go pick up Jerry's gun so we could test-fire it, compare it with shells that were found at the scene.
Q. Did he give you a search warrant or anything like that?
A. No.
Q. What time did you go to Jerry's home on the 10th?
A. Approximately 3 p.m.
Q. Three p.m. that afternoon?
A. Yes.

"In the morning", "in the afternoon", "it was behind the trailer", "it was in front" ... There were a lot of questions asked and answered in the two-day trial. Not always the same answer by different people and not always the same answer by the same person within minutes apart. If there is ever a question why I refer to this story as <u>Sins of Henry County</u>, there is the answer. I would love to have the names of every juror who sent Jerry Banks to the electric chair. Let's get it out in the open and on the record right here. I don't like what I found in the Sheriff's Office, the D.A.'s Office, the jury or from the bench. And I'm still not sure what I think of the press.

There was one very important question in which Attorney Hudson John Myers asked almost everyone on the police force.
Q. Did you or do you know who took Jerry Banks home the morning of November 8th at 5 a.m.
A. No.

Pay attention! They can't remember!
Not one person would answer that question. And that bothered me. I am willing to bet any amount of money it was not Sgt. Tommy Floyd. And if given that bet, I would put all of my winnings on Det. Dick Barnes and Det. Paul Robbins as the two who drove Jerry Banks home that morning.

I'm sorry if it seems like I'm dropping bread crumbs. Just dog ear this page, you'll be coming back.

Now all of the above is a portion of the trial testimony from trial #2. I read all of that and tons of other statements two dozen times and I thought "these are the dumbest questions on earth to be asking while a man's life is hanging in the balance." To be honest with you, it was near the end of the book that I happened to pick up the trial records and started reading them again. What a difference! The testimony above is the most telling of all. The same dumb questions by Hudson John Myers, over and over; I could not see where he was going. Now as I read his words, he knew much more than he could state in court. Attorney Myers would have been out of line asking a question, point-blank about his suspicions, so the next best thing would be to have them on record as making conflicting statements under oath in court. Am I picking sides here? No! You'll still have to decide for yourself.

Counsel's advice to me was also that I should not say anything I cannot prove to be an undeniable fact. Jerry Banks said "I picked it [the wallet] up from the ground" and then "I took it out of his back pocket." Then he said "I loaned my gun to another man. He must have kill'em". Then he told them he made that up because he wanted to get them off his back. Basically he was scared to death of dying in the electric chair for something he didn't do. And that made him not only a liar but a murder suspect. If conflicting statements from Jerry Banks made him a liar, then why doesn't conflicting statements, from Detectives Phillip Howard, Dick Barnes, Paul Robbins and Sheriff Glass, make all of them liars, also? Why not murder suspects? Or maybe the liars were Andrew Lake Eberhardt and County Commissioner Bud Kelley. So! Who were the liars? I will tie all the above <u>underlined</u> statements together later and you will see. Dog ear this page too. We haven't heard from County Commissioner Bud Kelley, yet.

Please allow me to share with you one more very interesting question directed to Lead Detective Howard. Attorney Myers saved this one for his last question.

BY MYERS:

> Q. What were the circumstances regarding your leaving the Sheriff's Department?

BY MR. McGARITY: Your Honor please, this doesn't have anything in the world to do with the investigation here before us, not one thing. Whether he went for a higher salary or ...

BY THE COURT: I don't see how it would be at this point. Do you contend that it is material?

BY MR. MYERS: Yes, Sir. I do.

BY THE COURT: Ladies and Gentlemen of the Jury, the court will let you go to the Jury room while I hear from the attorneys on a point of law.

Attorney Hudson Myers did not get what he wanted. He felt if he could convince Judge Sosebee, he would be allowed to continue this line of questioning with the Jury present. So he explained to the Judge that he felt that Howard's leaving the department was directly related to the issues at hand.

"I believe that the testimony is material and that it relates to the investigation at the time, which Detective Howard was head of ... It relates, the circumstances of his leaving may relate to the disposition of that investigation, the nature of the investigation and the ... if, in fact ... the circumstances of his leaving related directly to the investigation that is now before the Court and the evidence being submitted to the jury; that in answering questions if there is a connection, then the answer would reveal that connection. If not, the answer would show there was no connection."

Mr. Craig complained almost whiningly before the Judge saying Mr. Myers' question should be limited to allow a "yes or no" answer. They did not want the Jury to hear anything about Howard's departure.

Restating the question and Howard giving an answer with a "No", the Jury returned hearing none of Myers' concerns.

Sherriff Jimmy Glass: First having been duly sworn, testified as following:

BY HUDSON JOHN MYERS:

Q. Do you recall seeing a Henry County citizen by the name of Andrew Lake Eberhardt on November 7th 1974, (the day of the murders) at approximately 6:30 p.m. on Old Rock Quarry Road?
A. I do not remember seeing Mr. Eberhardt.
Q. Have you had the opportunity since November 7th, 1974 to meet and talk to a Henry County citizen by the name of Andrew Lake Eberhardt?
A. I have.
Q. How many occasions have you seen or talked to Andrew Lake Eberhardt since November 7th 1974?
A. Only twice that I remember.
Q. Can you give us the dates of the first occasion?
A. I cannot give you the date; he called and said he had some information that was available; it was after the first trial.
Q. That was on the telephone?
A. That was on the telephone.
Q. Now, when was the second time you had occasion to talk or meet with him?
A. When he came into my office the day after our phone conversation.
Q. Do you remember the approximate date of that?
A. It was after the first trial.

✧ ✧ ✧

Andrew Lake Eberhardt: First having been duly sworn, testified as following:

BY HUDSON JOHN MYERS:

Q. Mr. Eberhardt now, while driving down the road, did you have the occasion to be stopped or flagged down by anyone that afternoon or evening?

A. Yes, I did.
Q. Would you tell us what you did after seeing this person attempting to flag you down?
A. Well, I almost didn't stop and then I figured that it might have been a hunting accident, so I stopped to see if I could see what the problem was.
Q. Well, why did you think that there might be a hunting accident?
A. Well, the gentleman had hunting gear and a gun with him and appeared to have been hunting and I knew people hunted in this area. The puppy was with him scampering around in the road.
Q. What did he say to you?
A. He said that he had found two people who had been shot in the woods and I asked him if they were dead and he said, yes, they were then he asked if I would call the police department and I told him, yes, I would.

Mr. Eberhardt went on to explain he drove several miles up the road and stopped to use the phone at the Matador Inn. After turning in, he realized he did not know where the phone was so he figured driving on to his house would be quicker. He told the court that it took several times before he got through because the line was busy. He told the person "on the phone" who he was. "Yes, Sir, I gave them my name, who I was and where I lived."

Mr. Eberhardt stated how he told the person on the phone everything that happened and said a black man was hunting and found the bodies. He told the court, "I told him the black man would be waiting by the road."

Q. What did you do after you hung up the telephone?
A. I decided that it had been a good while since I had first stopped on the road side and that he might think that I had not called anyone. He indicated ... when he first stopped me he indicated that he had stopped a car previous to me and that they said that they didn't want to get involved.
Q. They did not want to get involved?
A. That was my understanding, yes. I forgot about that and then I figured that he might think I didn't want to get involved either, so it was getting toward dark and cool that evening and I got my hat and my coat and my son to go with me and we went back over to Hudson Road and back down the Rock Quarry Road.

Andrew Lake Eberhardt explained this trip took him five to ten minutes to get to his house and maybe a half hour to make the call and load up again and another five to ten minutes to return.

Q. When you arrived at the place where this man stopped you, was he still there and was he alone?
A. He and his little dog that was with him ... were still there.

BY THE COURT: (JUDGE SOSEBEE)

Q. You didn't answer his question. Mr. Eberhardt was he alone?
A. Yes, he was by himself.

I just don't seem to get it! "Was he alone?" "He and his little dog that was with him ...." Judge Sosebee thought if Jerry Banks was only with his dog, he must have been alone. I know I'm off track here but, hell the dog was the one who found the bodies. You're never alone when you're with a dog, ever!

Eberhardt went on to tell the court two officers, one he remembered as being a colored man were the first to arrive. That would have been Detectives Tomlinson and Dick Barnes. Eberhardt said it was getting dark and he could tell the police couldn't see very well so he told them, he was going back to his house and get his Coleman lantern. He did and he returned, filled it with fuel and pumped it up, lit it and the officers used it while they processed the crime scene.

> Q. While your lantern was in use and down in the wood, did you have the occasion on November 7, 1974, to talk to Jimmy Glass?
> A. When he came up and went into the woods, I didn't talk to him at first. While they were still doing things out there ... whatever they were doing, he came out of the woods, started up the street to leave and I went up to him at that time and told him who I was and that I had married one of the Austin girls, thinking the fact that they had gone to school together might ... I don't know ... was ... something we had in common, and I mentioned that and he said he was going somewhere to a speaking engagement was the reason he was leaving.
> Q. Did you ever have the occasion to make any other phone calls?
> A. I called the week that the information came in the newspaper that the trial date was scheduled. I called again and talked with Sheriff Glass and told him if they were going to need me to testify that I would appreciate having some notice because I travel from time to time in my job and that I had planned to be in Tennessee that week.
> Q. And what was his reply?
> A. That he didn't think they would need my testimony.

Well, that pretty well sums it up for me. I feel like Sheriff Jimmy Glass didn't seem to care about the truth or helping Jerry Banks. That is, unless I could be convinced Andrew Lake Eberhardt was a bold-face liar.

> Q. Was there a third occasion that you had an opportunity to speak with Sheriff Glass?
> A. When I arrived back from Tennessee that week, my wife showed me the Atlanta paper saying that Mr. Banks had been convicted and sentenced to death and that they still ... someone testified that they didn't know who I was, on

the stand, and that upset me and I worried about it all weekend and then I went on the following Monday morning with my son down to Jackson (Georgia) to see Judge Sosebee and I didn't know what else to do.

Q. And what did you tell Judge Sosebee?

A. That I was under the impression that the Sheriff's Department knew who I was and that I made no effort to keep myself from being known and that among my friends and people in the community, I had ... that the thing had been discussed and that I had made no effort for them not to know that I was the one that stopped. Judge Sosebee told me that he would take care of notifying the proper people and I returned home and I got to thinking about it and I figured that maybe I better call Sheriff Glass again and tell him I'd been to see Judge Sosebee and I did and he asked me to come down at that time and make a statement the following morning to him.

Q. And this is Sheriff Glass?

A. Yes, Sir.

Q. And what time did you go to see Sheriff Glass the following morning?

A. Early in the morning, nine, ten, something along in there.

Q. And did you take anyone with you?

A. My brother-in-law, Robert Austin, went with me.

Q. Why did you take Mr. Austin with you?

A. I was under the impression that they were a little unhappy with me after I talked to Sheriff Glass over the telephone and I just was apprehensive about it and my brother-in-law knew him and I thought that things would maybe be a little nicer if Robert were with me.

Q. What, if anything, did Sheriff Glass tell you at that meeting?

A. We talked about the fact that he had had several ...

BY MR. CRAIG: Your Honor please, I think that we have gotten past the point where anything that may have any influence on

this trial. We have already passed ... Mr. Eberhardt is obviously here now and ...
BY THE COURT: Well, let me send the Jury to the room.
BY MR. MYERS: Your Honor, that won't be necessary; I'll withdraw the question and I am through questioning this witness.
The Defense rests.

This oversight by someone failing to remember Eberhardt of course was the reason Banks was even given the second trial. I thought it odd that Judge Sosebee felt this was important enough to look into but during a hearing held in March of 1975, Sosebee felt it was not important enough for Jerry to be given a new trial.

⊕ ⊕ ⊕

CHAPTER 10

The 2nd Verdict

At times, I think the jury had no choice but to find Banks guilty because the evidence was against him. Does that change the way I feel? Hell no!

To better understand why the verdict was incorrect, it is important to study the time line. Time ... time is the most important aspect of the case for understanding what took place that November day in 1974. I read it over and over, looked at every word, wrote down the time line, the names of everyone, every date and the time of every event. Then one day I started seeing the picture from a "new perspective", the perspective of possibilities and impossibilities.

From the GBI Crime Laboratory, Mr. Fite was a micro analyst, and it was his job to examine physical evidence in all of its aspects. With a B.S. Degree in Chemistry and Mathematics from Berry College in Rome, Georgia, Mr. Fite had been with the Crime Lab for almost 8 years. He was their expert.

The killings were on the 7th (Thursday) and the first two evidence shells in question were said to be found sometime around 7:00 a.m. to 9:00 a.m. on (Friday) the 8th.

The day of November the 9th (Saturday) was the day the two evidence rounds were taken to the Lab.

Kelly Fite on the stand, being questioned by the Prosecutors about the shotgun shells found at the scene and his determination of the type gun that fired those shells.

Q. Were you able to determine what type of weapon they were fired from?
A. Well, I examined these cartridge casings on the November 9th and I found no evidence of these cartridge casings having been fired in any type repeating weapon or bolt action.
Q. What do you mean by repeating weapon?
A. A self-loading weapon, an automatic or pump or a bolt action or a single-shot bolt action.
Q. Single-shot bolt action?
A. Yes, this left only the break-top, single and double-barrel shotgun.

Self-loading type guns leave marks on the brass base of the casing by the mechanism in the gun which pushes each round into the chamber. There were no such marks on the evidence shells meaning the only type of gun left was "a manual-loading type" in which the shell is loaded by hand and leaves a different type of marks when ejected.

A break-top shotgun's barrel hinges down when opened to load or unload a shell or shells in the case of a double-barrel gun.

Next, Kelly Fite was questioned about State's Exhibit #20, the three test-fired shells that Detective Phillip Howard fired from Jerry's gun on (Sunday) November 10, 1974. Kelly Fite said he received those shells on December 2, 1974, and compared them to Exhibit #19, the shells found at the scene.

Q. And what were the results of your comparison?
A. Well, I found that #20 and #19 exhibited identical breach face markings and firing pin impressions.
Q. Is this done with the naked eye or how?
A. Well, I have a comparison microscope at the Crime Laboratory and it's really two microscopes breached together and when you look through the eye pieces of this microscope, you see two objects, one under each scope

divided only by a hairline. This scope has varying magnification for approximately ten-power up to about three hundred. It also has a fiber optic system so the examiner can adjust the lighting to his desired angle. I used this microscope to compare State's Exhibits #19 and #20."

Kelly Fite went on to state that he had Banks' shotgun brought to the laboratory and he test fired two rounds himself and they also matched identically to the shell casings found at the murder scene, Exhibit #19.
During the 2nd trial, examination of Kelly Fite by Mr. Craig: Mr. Craig was interrupted.

BY THE COURT:

Q. Do you know whether that shotgun will eject a shell?
A. Sir, in my test with the State's Exhibit #1 (Jerry Banks' gun), it functioned as a shotgun of this age and condition would; it did eject the cartridge case. It pushes them back instead of ejects [sic] them.
Q. So it will push it back where you can reach and pull it out?
A. You can pull it out, yes, sir.

I did not like Mr. Fite's answer to that question the first time I read it. I was surprised Attorney Hudson Myers had not objected. To a juror inexperienced about guns, this answer gave the impression the user of that gun would have the option of pulling the shell out. Like there wasn't really anything wrong with Jerry's gun. Look at his first answer, "... it did eject the cartridge case. It pushes them back instead of ejects them." First he states "it did eject them", then in the same breath, "It pushes them back instead of ejects [sic] them." If that gun operated properly, when you broke it down, opening the barrel, the gun would eject the shell casing onto the ground allowing you to quickly insert another shell.

He was asked, "Do you know whether that shotgun will eject a shell?" In other words, did the gun operate properly? Kelly Fite did not answer the question. And that question came from the Judge and he was a stickler for getting questions answered.

From this "new perspective" I studied the closeness of the bodies and the first two shots and how they had to be fired very close together, not only in distance between each victim but more importantly in the timing between each shot. This was crucial. Basically, the longer the time between the shots could increase the distance between the victims and the location of the second pool of blood.

See Figure 9: Reconstruction of Crime Scene. There were two victims standing near the back of Marvin King's car with someone behind them with a shotgun, their backs to Quarry Road and the pine thicket to their right and they knew they were about to die. The two pools of blood were beside each other, but King's (on the left) was further away from the gun than Miss Hartsfield's (on the right) by three or four feet. Doctor Howard from the GBI testified there was no evidence of any restraint devices used on either victim. When they fell away from the shooter, their heads were even farther away. By the size of the entry wounds to their heads, it is apparent that the killer may have moved a bit closer to make his final two shots.

However, it seems to me Melanie Hartsfield's first wound in the back was the closest to the gun and therefore, the only wound to retain evidence about the unique type of shells used to kill them. The order of the murders is still uncertain. **See Figure 6: State Exhibit 2: The Two Pools of Blood.** Notice the left pool has a smaller spot of blood off to the side. That was from Marvin King's elbow. Miss Hartsfield, on the right was closer to the gunman.

It is my opinion that King was on the left side (of the killer) and turned to his right as a last chance to stay alive. Before he turned completely around, BAM the first shot was fired, hitting King in the right elbow, going through it and into his right side, knocking him to the ground. BAM, a second shot right behind the first hit Miss Hartsfield in her lower back, knocking her to the ground next to King. According to Doctor Howard from the GBI, the first shot for each victim was deadly, however Marvin King's would not have been instant death. While on the ground, Miss Hartsfield was shot behind the right ear exiting the top of her head. While Marvin King was still alive, he was shot dead center in the back of his head and exited his forehead.

I can't understand the killer's motive yet, as he stands there in control. It is possible the killer wanted Marvin King to know Miss Hartsfield was going to die first and he wanted Marvin King to watch her die. I propose this as just something to think about. As the first round exploded taking Hartsfield down, Marvin King would have turned to his right quickly and within seconds, he would get hit in the right elbow, as he could only rotate a quarter of a turn.

Either way, regardless of the order of the shootings, you cannot reload a single shot break-top shotgun that fast, even with a brand-new shotgun. Meaning, if Miss Hartsfield had been shot first, Marvin King would have had plenty of time to attack anyone trying to reload an old gun in the condition of Jerry's. It wouldn't eject the shell casing.

By the same token Melanie Hartsfield would not have stood there waiting to die. I believe one of the blood spots would have been much farther away from the other.

Time is everything, particularly when you're about to die. I guess the jury was thinking that Marvin King turned to see if Jerry needed any help reloading that old broken shotgun!

Under normal circumstances, it would have taken Jerry Banks five seconds at the least to reload that gun. On top of that, I got to thinking about the other three shotgun shells. If Jerry Banks had fired the first round, he would have had one hand near the trigger, and the other holding the barrel. In order to reload, he would have to keep his right hand near the trigger while using his left hand to hit the release to open the breech. Then Jerry would have had to "pull the fired shell out of the gun" throwing it away and then insert a new round. All of this time while holding the other shells in his ... third hand or in his pocket. Then close the breech and support the barrel, pull the trigger and fire, all under 5 seconds. Either way would have taken too much time.

✧ ✧ ✧

It is not my thinking that the killer planned that very spot. I think a simple walk over to the area of the pine trees was the first choice. That way the bodies would have been hidden and the dragging of the two bodies over a hundred feet away would not have been necessary.

Observe the crime scene photographs. **See Figure 6: State Exhibit #2: The two Pools of Blood.** I have gone over this photograph more than any that were taken. This picture alone tells more about what happened and what could not have happened that day. It tells me about time and what could and could not happen in that time. It tells about strength or the lack of strength on Jerry Banks' part, what he could or could not have done.

Notice how close the pools of blood are to each other. This relates to the time issue I spoke about. Notice the smeared blood from the dragging of the body to the right. That was Melanie's body leaving those marks. You can clearly see where her face cut into the dirt, removing her blood.

Yes, Jerry Banks could have picked up her feet and pulled her body a hundred feet or more. But observe the other blood spot belonging to Marvin King with the smaller spot of blood from his elbow. You don't see any evidence of King being dragged to the woods in the same manner. There is a slight smear of blood where his body touched the ground. I believe he was picked up by at least two people and carried a portion of the way, then dragged the remainder of the way. Jerry Banks only weighed 165 pounds, while King was 180. Even if it were possible for Jerry to have carried King, he and his clothing would have been covered with blood. Jerry Banks was not the killer.

See Figure 10: The Two Pools of Blood with the Body Layout. You will see I have outlined the bodies with respect to the blood on the ground. Keep in mind the victims were face down when they were shot in the back of their heads.

The first time I made the drawing, the bodies were 180 degrees in the other direction. Their feet were pointed in the other direction. I did that because that was the only way I could line up King's right elbow with the smaller blood spot off to one side. After examining the layout, I realized it was all wrong. Observing the blood from Melanie Hartsfield, you can see evidence where her body was dragged to the right which would be in the direction of the pine thicket. The problem with that layout was they would have been dragged by their arms. Doctor Howard from the GBI stated they were dragged by their feet.

Now with their feet in the proper direction as shown in the body layout drawing, this would have been the proper position for the bodies lying on the old road bed. I felt relieved that I had produced the layout of the crime that night.

But there was one problem. With this layout Marvin King's left elbow is over the blood spot. There was no other layout possible which would put his right elbow in place and their feet in their proper direction, so I came to the conclusion, that as soon as the fourth shot was fired, Marvin King was quickly rolled over on his back. This position would place his right elbow as shown, to begin bleeding out as a separate blood spot.

I have not made a reference to a hit-man earlier. I do now. It is my belief that Marvin King was rolled over allowing a picture to be taken of him. It is not inconceivable that proof of death would be needed in getting a quick payment for a murder. The crime scene photographs of the bodies shows a large amount of blood on Mr. King's back as well as the back side of his right arm. He was left on his back for some time.

One last thought in my process of trying to connect Jerry Banks and Marvin King in any way. **See Figures 12 and 13: Back side of Marvin King's Bloody Hands.** You can see how bloody Marvin King's hands were. Both victims were pulled by their feet into the woods. I was puzzled why only his hands were so bloody. Mr. King was picked up originally, not dragged. You wouldn't pick up a 180-pound man by his hands. But even if that were the case, was the blood transferred from the killer? There was no blood transferred to Melanie's hands. I see no reason why the killer would have that much or any blood on him, anyway. Then I noticed the UGA ring on Marvin King's right-hand finger and what appeared to be his wedding ring on his left. I remembered testimony about his hand being swollen during his autopsy.

I reverted to the trial testimony:

BY MR. MYERS: (Defense Attorney)

> Q. Officer Barnes, you indicated on direct examination that you were able to identify the victims from their jewelry that were on their person, is that correct?

A. That's correct. ...
Q. Now, that (his University of Georgia ring) was located on his right or left hand?
A. I'm not sure.
Q. And did you follow up on the initials in the ring that has been identified as that belonging to Marvin King?
A. No, sir ... I believe it was ... the ring from Mr. King was removed at the funeral home, so I believe Detective Robbins and Dr. Howard removed the ring. The ring was swollen on the finger and they worked together to remove it.

From this testimony and the photos of Mr. King's hands, I believe he fought for his life. The knuckles on both hands were bloodied and swollen. His left hand had an open wound. I have stated before there were some anger issues involved in this murder. There was a score to be settled. Someone, somewhere had blood on them also and they could have gone to work the next day with a fat lip. Again Jerry Banks had neither.

✥ ✥ ✥

Attorney Myers never spoke about any motive. He never put forth to the jury any questions about Jerry Banks' old style gun. These were the kind of things that Attorney Myers should have preached to the jury. These were the things the District Attorney, Judge Sosebee, and the jury, as well as the news reporters, should have taken into consideration.

As it turned out, the time it would have taken for Jerry to fire, reload, fire again, reload, and fire over and over again was not completely lost by the jury. This was one of the aspects of the case which made the strongest impression on them. In fact it was the length of time it took between the first two shots that awarded Jerry Banks the death sentence. The jury had not fallen completely asleep but they didn't view that evidence with any common sense. I mentioned time was the most important factor in this case. Well in the minds of the Jury, the lengthy time taken to unload, reload, re-aim, and re-fire the gun was a cruel, inhumane and a vile act for the second victim. For this, they gave Jerry Banks the death penalty. I'm not liking what I have learned about either jury.

⊕ ⊕ ⊕

The reason Detective Howard said he had Officer Barnes pick up Jerry's shotgun on the Sunday, 10th of November was so he could test fire his gun. Barnes said, "The following Sunday (after the murders) I went and picked the shotgun up at Jerry Banks' residence for the purpose of test firing for comparison of ballistics." He explained that Detective Howard fired three rounds into a pile of dirt by the trailer. Officer Barnes was sure about everything except when the shotgun was returned to Jerry. He did not know how long Detective Howard had the gun or who returned the gun. How, when and who returned the gun to Jerry or Perry Banks has never been ascertained.

Detective Phillip Howard testified a half dozen times that he did test fire the gun on Sunday, November 10, 1974. He was very sure of that and Detective Barnes was as well. When Detective Paul Robbins took the stand he supported their testimony. Paul Robbins testified to witnessing Lead Detective Howard firing State's Exhibit #1. He said "I was in the trailer when he took the shotgun outside. It was in the afternoon on Sunday because I remember saying something to Howard about this was going to interrupt church services." He stated immediately after that he heard loud noises ... "three reports from the shotgun".

⊕ ⊕ ⊕

Earlier in the trial:

After being questioned at length by Hudson John Myers, Officer Barnes was questioned on re-direct by Attorney Ed McGarity for the Prosecution. His only question was if that dog (of Jerry's) looked like a deer-hunting dog. "It wasn't a deer-dog, was it?"

He was inferring that Jerry must have killed those people if he claimed to be deer hunting with a puppy. He made it sound as though Jerry was lying about hunting that day. Jerry Banks was hunting that day, he was rabbit hunting and rabbit hunters do not use 00 buck ammunition. They kept on insinuating Jerry was deer hunting and used 00 buck ammunition.

Q. At the time you arrived at the scene, did you see the dog there?
A. Yes, sir.
Q. What size dog was it?
A. It was a small.
Q. A small puppy?
A. Yes.
Q. It wasn't a deer-dog, was it?
A. No, sir.

I have not read anywhere of any officer stating in court that they were ever told by Banks that he was deer hunting. I was told by several people he was rabbit hunting. First of all, if Jerry Banks had been deer hunting, it would not have been at 2:30 in the afternoon. No one goes deer hunting in the middle of the day.

On the other hand, if Jerry Banks had been rabbit hunting with Winchester Western XX Super X 00 Buck, Mark V, 12-gauge shells, there would not have been enough rabbits within five miles to make a decent meal ... because (00) double ought buckshot is the most powerful and the most destructive shotgun ammunition on the market. Hence Jerry Banks would have needed a whole lot of rabbits. Winchester Western XX Super X 00 Buck, Mark V, 12-gauge shells were used by the military and law enforcement, which makes it an even more powerful round.

There were so many unanswered questions that came to mind as I read over the files. No officer ever asked or looked to see what type shell Jerry had on him. Not once. Not one officer ever checked Jerry's clothes for blood splatter.

The 2nd Verdict

✣ ✣ ✣

The bullpen had been Jerry's home for nearly a year by the end of the second trial. One thing Sheriff Jimmy Glass did was allow Perry and Ludie Banks to bring Virginia to see Jerry. Perry said they would drive her down to the jail on early Saturday mornings around two or three a.m. Glass would allow Virginia to visit at night and she would be taken home around six in the morning. Perry and I often wondered why Jimmy Glass allowed this. I do have my ideas.

✣ ✣ ✣

The jury had heard all the evidence and they and their task were finished. By the end of November of 1975 this case was officially over and Jerry Banks made the headlines again. After the second trial, Jerry Banks was sentenced to die for the second time. This time he was ordered to die in Georgia's electric chair in Jackson, Georgia, just twenty miles south of McDonough, but he remained in the bullpen for a while longer.

CHAPTER 11

Relevant Facts and Dates

If anyone were to read over the original trial testimony, there wouldn't be anything to jump off of the pages like in a Mickey Spillane novel, but it is there. I am sure I'm not the first to read these records. If I copied the trial transcripts and put a title to them and called it a book, it's possible you could read it and never see what was before your eyes. But I didn't just read them; I studied them, word for word, over and over again, many times. This is why I repeat details and then try to paint a picture. This chapter will go over major and minor details of the trial testimony, which are the foundation of my claims.

RELEVANT FACT #1:

It was stated in court by Det. Dick Barnes that on November 10, 1974, three days after the murders, Detective Phillip Howard sent him to Banks' home to acquire his shotgun for test firing. Detective Phillip Howard testified it was in the morning. Detective Barnes testified it was in the afternoon. Under oath, Lead Detective Howard said he fired three test rounds into a pile of dirt changing the location three different times. These three shell casings became State Exhibit #20, but he did not send them to the State Crime Laboratory until December 2, this was 23 days

later. Defense Attorney Hudson John Myers asked "What did you do with the gun after you had test fired it?" Detective Dick Barnes said, "Later the gun was returned to Jerry Banks ..."
On December 2, 1975, Detective Paul Robbins delivered State Exhibit #20, three Remington Peters 12-gauge shell casings, test fired by Detective Howard, 23 days after the test fire.

Why did this take so long? I think there were several reasons. Let me just say, I have to be careful about what I say and how I say it, and there are some things I better not say here. The drive to the GBI Lab from Henry County is maybe 45 minutes. I will go so far as to say I believe Detective Howard was waiting for the dust to settle before offering the test-fired shells to the GBI.

Relevant fact #2:

The day of December 13, 1975, over a month after the murders, another search party was formed. Detective Howard, Detective Paul Robbins, Sgt. Tommy Floyd, and Officer Bill Hart along with Captain J. B. Berry of the Clayton County police were part of this group. But that's not all; also invited were two officers from the GBI Crime Lab, Ed Jones and another Howard, Jim Howard.

This search party proved to be a success again. They located a third shell, State Exhibit #18. That round was found by Officer Bill Hart. He marked the shell with an "E" on the inside of the shell then handed that shell over to the State.

Boy that worked out well. I mean, think about it. Six weeks had gone by since the shooting and Jerry Banks had been arrested. They already had two shell casings that came from Jerry Banks' gun. To top it off Lead Detective Howard called for another search.

Could it have been that Lead Detective Phillip Howard was just playing it safe or covering his bases? Either way, you have to admit, having all of those outsiders witness the finding of another shell that was ultimately traced to Jerry Banks' shotgun, really took away any possible question about any improper chain of custody as to the first two shells. You know... just being on the safe side.

"Hide the thimble?" I think that's what went on that day.

If you are a baby-boomer, long before X-boxes, children would play a game with their mother's thimble. A thimble is a metal protective cap that women put over the tip of their finger while sewing. Children would form a circle with one player in the center with the thimble. All children would place their hands folded and pointed out as though they were praying. Each child would open their hands just enough to allow the one in the center to draw their folded hands through theirs and maybe drop the thimble into their hands. It doesn't matter where in the world this game was played, every child would smile if they received the thimble or not. This made it difficult to tell who had the thimble, which turns this event into a real guessing game.

I don't know, but to me it looked a lot like somebody was placing the thimble in the hands of the GBI while everybody was smiling.

Now this is where small details leave big impressions. I'm not one to let little things go unnoticed. The officer who found that third shell that day was Officer Bill Hart, a Henry County Sheriff's employee, but when he testified during the second trial, he was working in Clayton County, and he was the only one who found a shell, who went to the trouble to mark it.

Was it because he was trying to throw a monkey wrench into the old thimble game? Did he suspect something that might require him to do this? Or was he in the game? I would really love to know why he quit working for Sheriff Jimmy Glass.

Keep in mind this area is about a mile or so from Jerry's house and this is a popular hunting spot, even so noted by the police on the stand. It was thought possible that Perry Banks had hunted that area before with that very same shotgun. So the shells they were finding could have been there all along. Even Kelly Fite, the ballistics expert, said he could not tell how old the shells were or how long they had been at the scene.

But to be honest with you, they could not have been left earlier by Jerry Banks. Perry Banks informed me November 7, 1974, was the first time Jerry had ever borrowed his shotgun to go hunting.

Relevant fact #3:

Does this seem odd to anyone other than me to wonder what happened to the fourth shell casing? *There were four gunshot wounds.*

"Why would anyone walk off with the fourth shell in their pocket?" I ask.

It would seem to me that anybody who would go to all the trouble to kill these people, hide the bodies, cover them up and move the victim's car ... Well ... why would someone just bend over and pick up three of the shells and then throw them 35 to 50 feet away, to be found anyway? Why not stick all of them in one's pocket?

I don't think any shotgun would eject a shotgun shell that far away. Jerry's wouldn't even push out of the gun.

I would bet money, if Detective Howard had fired four rounds with Jerry's gun behind the court house, they would have found all four shells at the scene. Let's think about this. On November 10, where did the number three come into play? Why did he fire the gun only three times? Why were there only three evidence shells found at the crime scene. Not pointing any fingers here, just spit-balling. You make up your own mind.

Relevant fact #4:

The next morning after the murder, Mr. King's car had been found about a mile or two away in a field. It was returned to the scene of the crime by the Sheriff's Department. **See Figure 13: State Exhibit #16: Marvin King's Opel Station wagon**. Mr. King's car had a light over the license plate that had been hit and a piece of the glass cover was missing. The missing piece of glass cover was found near the site of all the blood. It was determined that Mr. King's car had been at the scene when the shotgun blast was fired. I believe a pellet struck King's bone at his elbow and ricocheted, when it hit the rear light cover on King's red Opel station wagon. Whoever the killer was moved the car afterwards.

The car belonging to Mr. King was gone over for prints by Clayton County investigators. As to the latent print report, the only finger-prints in Mr. King's car were those of the two victims.

Jerry's prints were never found anywhere.

By Tommy Floyd:

A. They were located on the rear-view mirror and on the inside of the vehicle. No prints were found outside the car.

By the Court: (Judge Sosebee)

Q. What about on the steering wheel?
A. No sir, none on the steering wheel.
Q. No readable prints on the steering wheel?
A. No readable prints, no sir.

Now three decades later, and I'm still confused about that steering wheel having prints on it even though they were not readable. The inside of the car was not wiped down in order to clean any prints otherwise there would not have been any prints on the steering wheel at all, readable or otherwise. There is a difference between latent prints, no readable prints and no prints at all. How could Banks have removed the blanket from the car and then drive the car two miles away and not leave his prints in or on the car? Someone was wearing gloves. This would have been the same as wiping the steering wheel but not totally clean.

The red bedspread wasn't mentioned in the first trial. During the second trial the police stated they had questioned Marvin King's wife, Mrs. Bobby King, and she said it was theirs. Maybe they withheld that information because the jury would have to conclude that Banks somehow removed the spread from Mr. King's car without leaving any prints on the outside or inside of the car even though it had not been wiped clean. Could that be possible? Yes! But that would have required Jerry to wear gloves and that would have required premeditation, planning and plotting in advance. They didn't want to go there.

Relevant Fact #5:

I ask you:

1. Why would Jerry Banks kill two people at 2:30 p.m.?
2. Not in the manner common to robberies, but more so of a contract hit or execution.
3. Then drag two bodies over 100 feet through heavy weeds into a pine thicket.
4. Go back and take a bedspread from the victim's vehicle to further hide the bodies.
5. Drive the vehicle two miles away and come back to the scene and sit around for three hours until 5:15 p.m.
6. Then start flagging down cars in order to get someone to help by calling the cops, so he could stand around another hour alongside of the road waiting for the police to come.
7. Then he could show the police how well he hid the bodies.
8. All the time holding a 12-gauge shotgun in his hand.

A very relevant set of facts are, how would Jerry Banks be able do all of this and not leave one finger print or have one single noticeable spot of blood on him or his clothing? Keep in mind, Marvin King was not dragged in the same manner as Melanie. If Jerry Banks had picked Marvin Kings' body up, he would have been covered in blood.

Relevant Fact #6:

The victims were from Clayton County and Clayton County police were told that Henry would handle the investigation. Clayton County detectives were given just enough information to make them think that Jerry Banks was their man. I know this for a fact because I have talked to Clayton County detectives, and they were kept in the dark. I know more about this case than they do. Information or evidence that would have been beneficial to Jerry Banks was withheld by certain people within the Sheriff's Department. Not only withheld from Clayton County authorities but from two juries and all six of Jerry Banks' lawyers, from 1975 until this day.

It is not my intention to suggest what facts were known or unknown by the Prosecutors' Office, or what knowledge that office may or may not have had about any details that were withheld from any of the Defense Attorneys for Jerry Banks.

Relevant fact #7:

Let's read from Sheriff Jimmy Glass's testimony during the second trial and pay attention to how the D.A. responded to these questions.

BY MR. MYERS: (To Sheriff Jimmy Glass)

Q. Do you recall on March 21st, 1975, (during a hearing for a second trial) a question that was posed on direct examination by Mr. Ed McGarity which he asked, "Have you withheld any evidence that would be beneficial to the defendant in the trial of this case?" Do you recall that question?
A. Yes, Sir, I recall it.
Q. Do you recall your answer?
A. To the best of my knowledge, my answer was that I have withheld no information in regards to this case.
By Mr. Myers: That's all, your Honor.

CROSS-EXAMINATION BY MR. CRAIG:

Q. Sheriff, in your duties ... your duties consist of day-to-day investigation of criminal matters, or is that done by some other department in the Sheriff's Office?
A. It's done by other departments.
Q. Your duties consist of those other than day-to-day investigations of criminal cases, is that right?
A. That is correct.

Now I had a phone conversation with Sheriff Jimmy Glass sometime around 2009 or 2010. This was after I might have told him a little tiny lie. I told him I was writing a book about the history of Henry County and his grandfather would be in it and I would enjoy talking to him also. Anyway, when I asked him about the Jerry Banks case, he assured me he had everything under control, nothing went on that he didn't know about. "I stayed on top of that case. I kept real close to that case, everything that went on." And I believe that to be a true fact.

I will cover the rest of my phone conversation with Sheriff Jimmy Glass in another Chapter.

Relevant fact #8:

Now I am going to tell you something that has never been spoken or written about publicly, ever. Perry Banks enlightened me with a family secret that Jerry Banks took to his grave. Jerry was not alone when the bodies were found on November 7, 1974. He had been hunting with cousin, Mamian Webster Jr. They found the bodies together.

Jerry and his cousin went hunting around 1:00 p.m. until sometime after 4:00 p.m. on November 7, 1974. On their way home at the end of the day they noticed the puppy had found something. It was two pools of fresh blood with drag marks in the direction of the pine thickets. There in a pine thicket covered with a red bedspread were two bodies, a white man and a young white girl. They removed the spread. I really don't think it was Jerry but one of the two removed the wallet from King's pocket or picked it up off the ground and discarded it in the woods. Jerry and his cousin Mamian had their discussion about what was the best thing for them to do. Jerry wanted to stay and Mamian wanted no part of it.

This is their paraphrased conversation according to what Perry Banks remembers from his conversation with his cousin Mamian Webster Jr., right after the murders.

"Jerry, let's get out of here, now."

"No, we've got to do something" Jerry said.

"Jerry, I'm telling you, let's get out of here. Those are white people and you don't want to get involved with this."

"I can't just leave them," Jerry said.

"I'm getting out of here. Come on, Jerry, please! They're going to put this on you."

Jerry stood there as his cousin backed up through the weeds and Jerry said, "You go on. Don't worry. I'll never say anything about you. I won't say anything. Don't worry. Go on."

"Jerry, they're going to put this on you. Please don't stay ... Jerry."

Mamian took off running and this was something Jerry could never tell anybody. Jerry had to remember that he was hunting alone that day.

Standing alongside Quarry Road with a shotgun and his puppy, he flagged down Mr. Eberhardt. He knew and he felt he was doing the right thing.

Perry Banks said, "Neither Jerry or I had spoken to Mamian since that day when Jerry was arrested." Jerry's cousin could have gone to the authorities and prevented Jerry from going to death row. He could have gotten himself locked up in the same cell as Jerry and they both would have died in the electric chair.

I spoke to Attorney Buddy Welch about this and he could not believe what I was saying. He said, "Where did you hear that?" If Jerry had ever told anyone about this, it would have been then Attorney Wade Crumbley, but even then Jerry would not allow his cousin to be implicated. That's the kind of person Jerry Banks was.

Relevant fact #9:

The only three things they could use to charge Jerry for the murders: (1) The three shells, (2) when he gave conflicting statements about the wallet and (3) for deer hunting with a non-regulation puppy.

Well, remember the inconsistent statements about the wallet. Once Jerry stated he took the wallet out of the victim's pocket and in another statement he said he picked it up off the ground near the pools of blood. Jerry Banks was caught telling two different stories.

I believe it was because he did not take the wallet. I believe he wasn't paying attention to Mamian, who did take the wallet; therefore he had to make up a story.

I have read Jerry Banks' testimony during the December 22, 1980 hearing. Jerry Banks had a good memory for details 6 years after the murders. Again, Jerry Banks lied to the police but it was because he just didn't know the truth. He was covering for his cousin Mamian Webster Jr.

The fact that Jerry told his cousin, "I can't leave these people like this," leads me to believe he didn't take the wallet. The reason I believe this is because it is the same reason I knew in 1974, when he was arrested. I knew he was innocent.

The truth of the matter is, I believe to this day if Jerry Banks had chosen to get out of bed and go fishing with a Zebco 33 and a basket of crickets, on November 7, 1974, they would have found a way to tie Jerry Banks to the murders, one way or another.

PART III:
EXHIBITS

State Exhibits:

#1. The defendants 12-gauge shotgun.
#2. Photograph of the two pools of blood.
#3. Warrant
#4, 5, 7, 8, 9, 10, 12, 13. All the Crime Scene photographs.
#6. The red bedspread.
#11. A missing person's report from Clayton County on Melanie Hartsfield.
#14. The red sweater and other articles of clothing removed from the female victim.
#15. Articles of clothing removed from the male victim.
#16. Photograph of male victim's car with broken tag light.
#17. Envelope containing a leather wallet with the initials, "W. K." on the face with a picture of Mrs. Bobby King inside.
#18. The third shell, also a Winchester Western 00 shotgun shell found on Dec. 13th during a search. State Exhibit #18 was handed over to the GBI.
#19. Two red Winchester Western 00 shotgun shells found at the scene by Detective Howard and Detective Ray on November 8th and said to have been delivered to the State Crime Lab by Detectives Paul L. Robbins and Tommy K. Floyd on the 9th of November.
#20. Three Remington Peters, 12-gauge shells from Jerry Banks' gun, test-fired by Phillip Howard behind the courthouse on Sunday, November 10, 1974, and delivered on December 2, 1975, by Paul L. Robbins to the State Crime Lab.
#21. Two shells test-fired by Kelly Fite at the State Lab on Dec. 6th.
#24. A small pillbox, containing wadding and pellets removed from the abdomen of the male victim.
#26. A small pillbox, containing wadding and pellets removed from the abdomen of the female victim.
#27. The portion of tag light from the male victim's car.

DEFENDANT'S EXHIBITS:

#1.   Unknown. It was not used in court.
#2.   A copy of the hand-written statement by Andrew Eberhardt.

Relevant Facts and Dates
MAPS AND PHOTOGRAPHS:

Figure 1
Jerry Banks: December 1980 with daughter Felicia and son Ed
Source: Family Photo

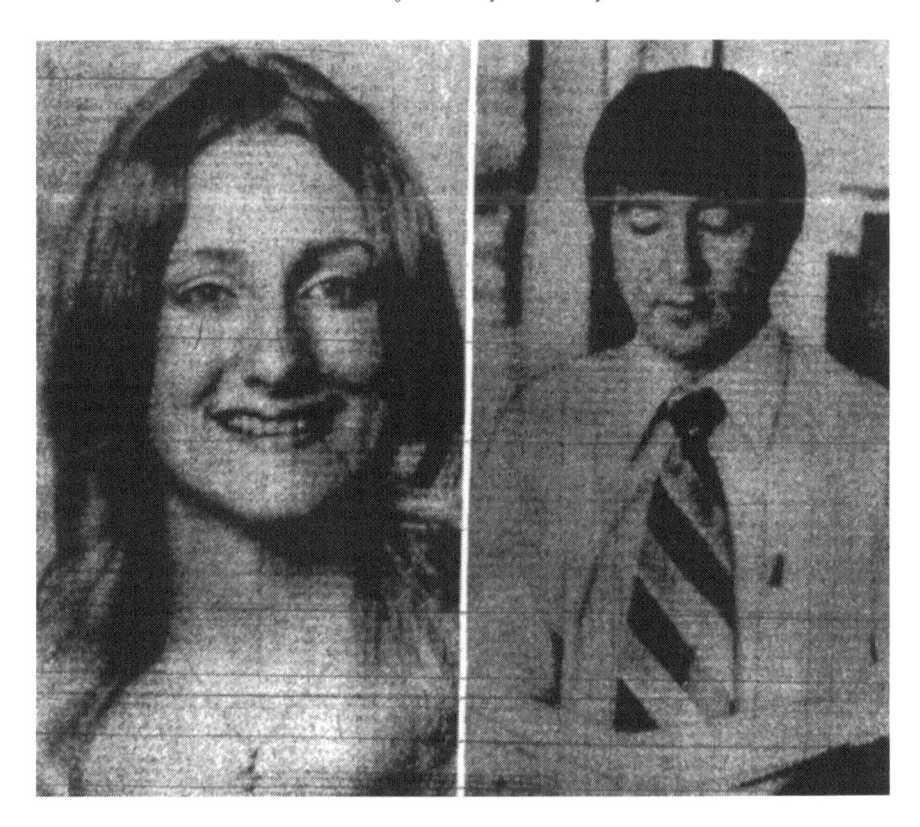

Figure 2 and 3
Melanie Ann Hartsfield and Marvin W. King
Source: Jonesboro High School, 1973 Year Book

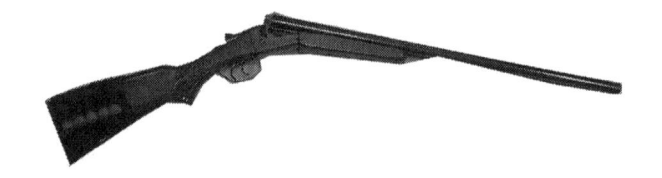

Figure 4
Stephens Arms break-top shotgun.
Source: Wikipedia, Stephens Arms

Relevant Facts and Dates

Figure 5
State Exhibit: Unknown: Aerial Photograph of Crime Scene
Source: Henry County Criminal Records Department

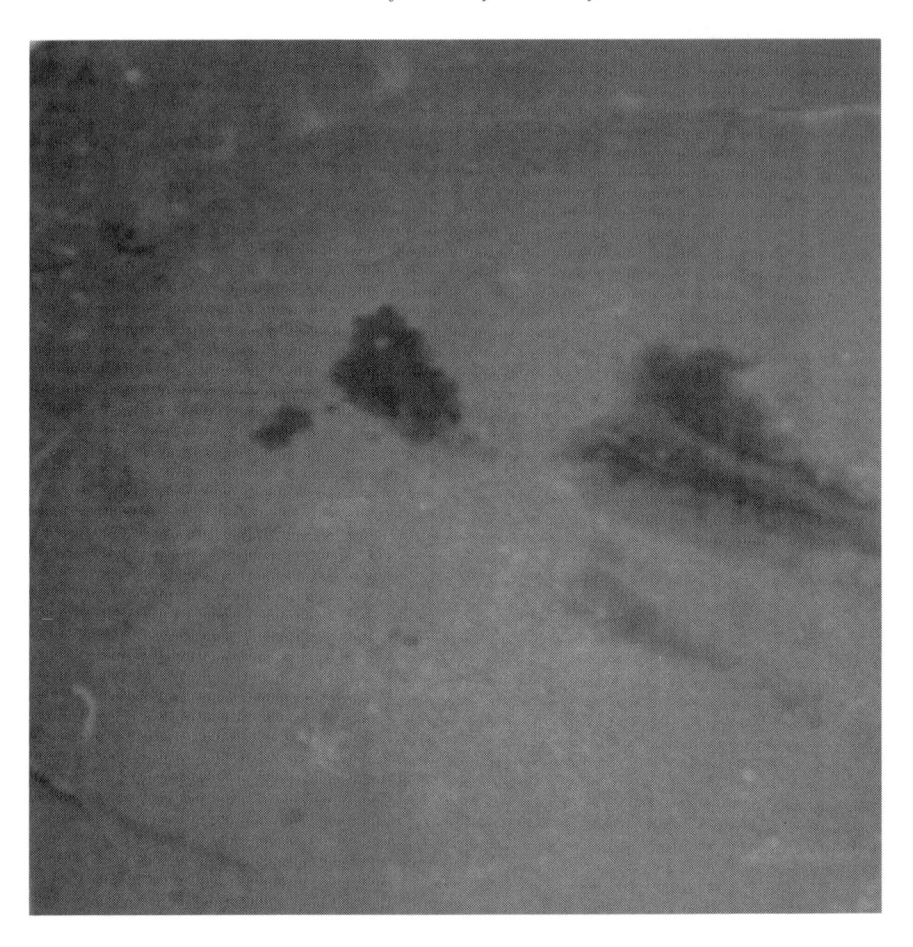

Figure 6
State Exhibit #2: The Two Pools of Blood.
Source: Henry County Criminal Records Department

Relevant Facts and Dates

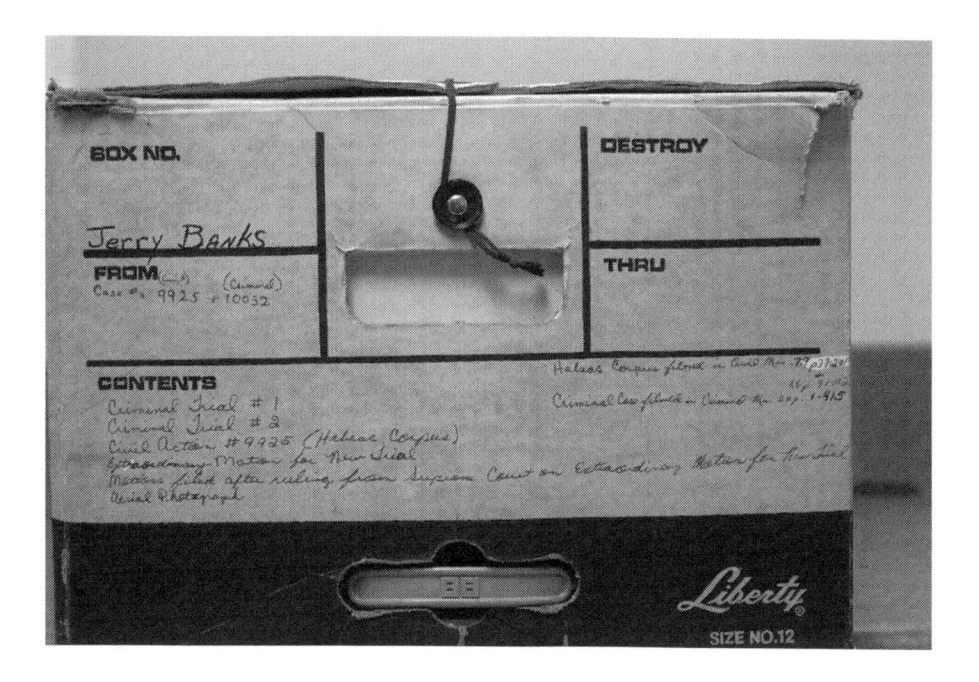

Figure 7
Court Documents: Georgia v. Banks
Source: Henry County Criminal Records Department

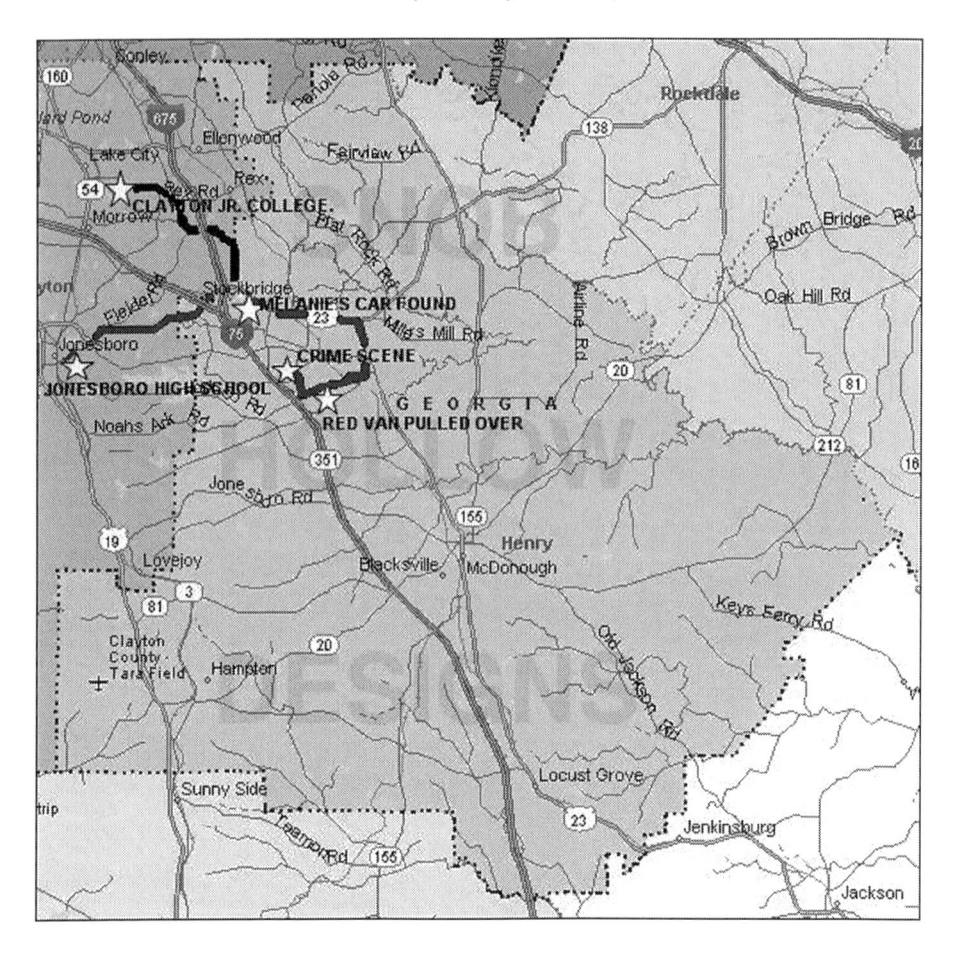

Figure 8
Routes Taken by Miss Hartsfield and Mr. King
Source: Online

Relevant Facts and Dates

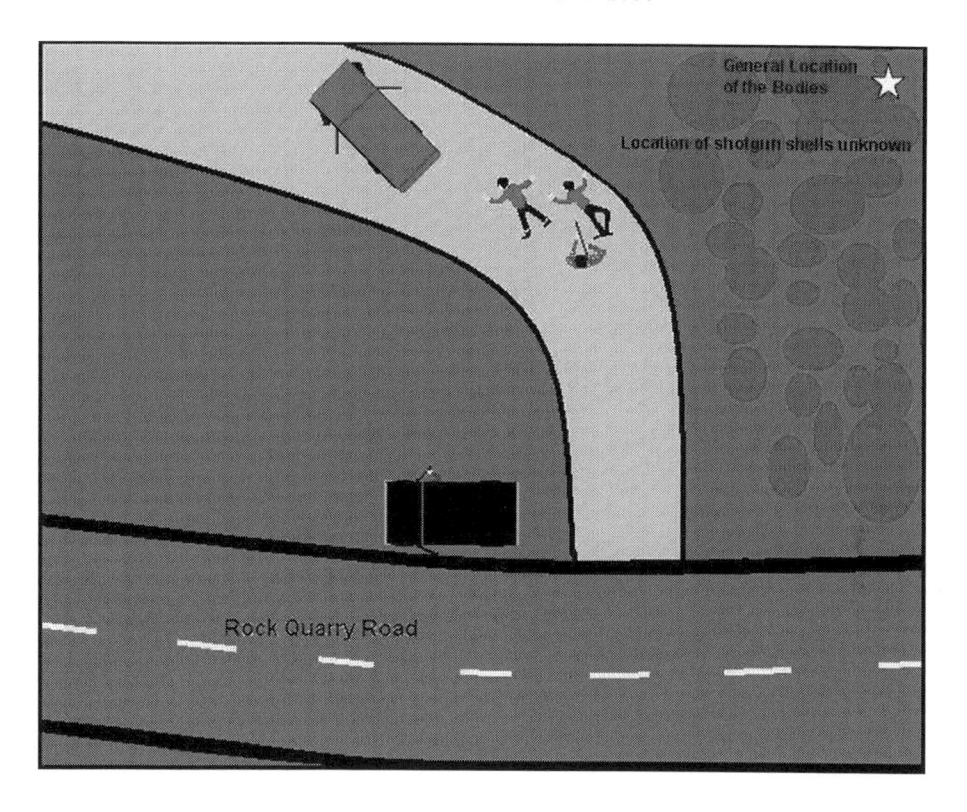

Figure 9
Reconstruction of Crime Scene
Source: Author's Drawing

Sins of Henry County

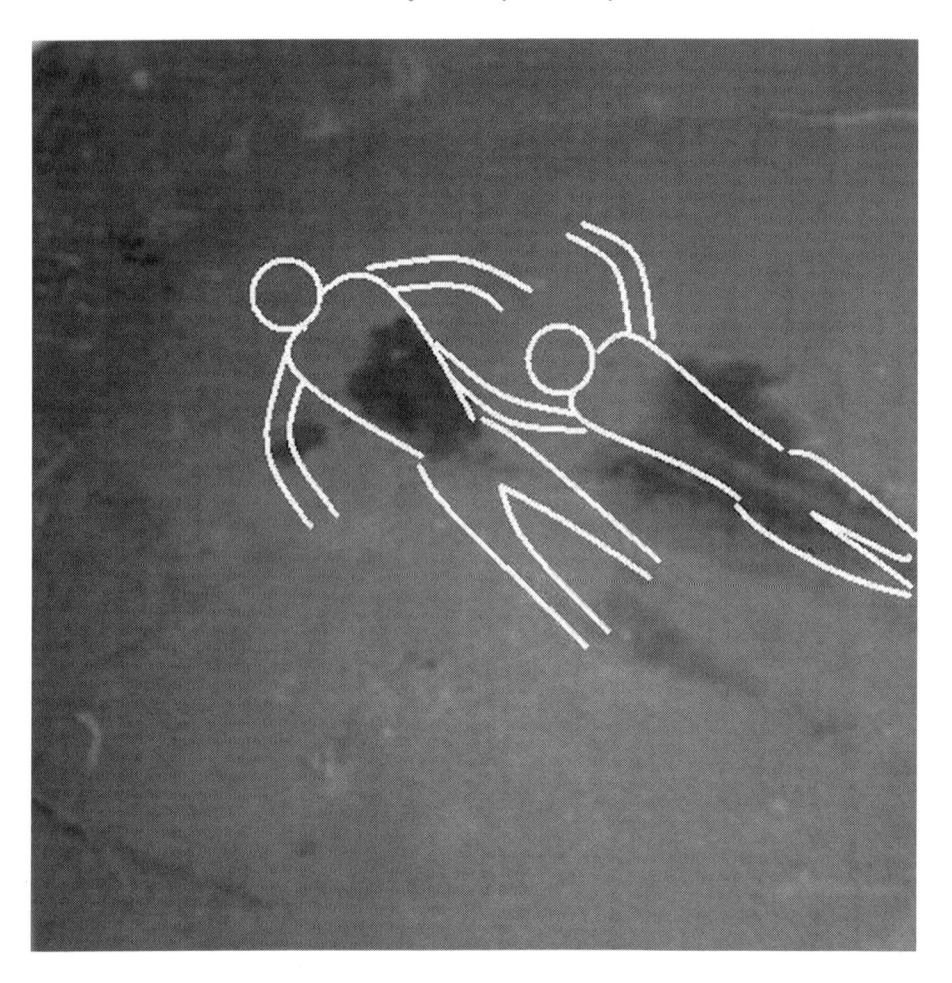

Figure 10
The Two Pools of Blood with the Body Layout
Source: Henry County Criminal Records Department

Relevant Facts and Dates

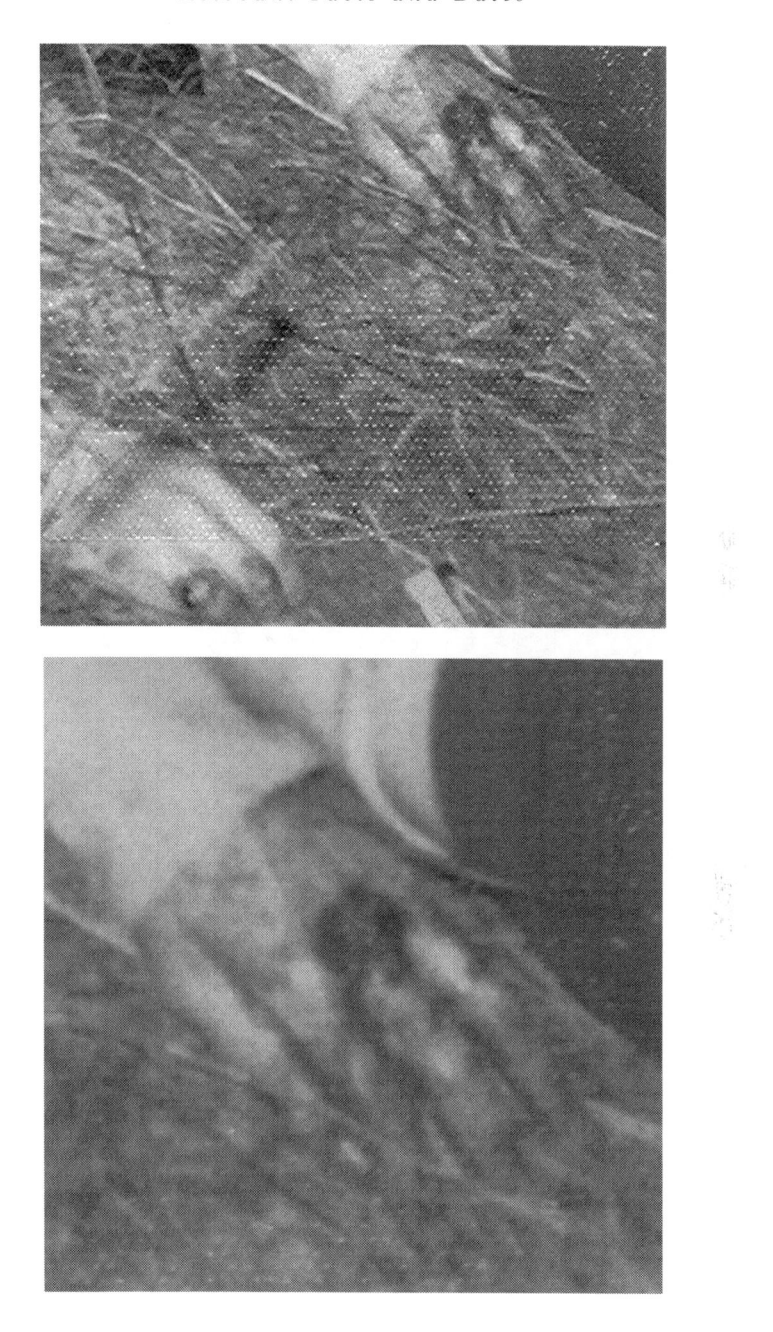

Figure 11 and 12
State Exhibit #4: Back side of Marvin King's Bloody Hands
Source: Henry County Criminal Records Department

Figure 13
State Exhibit #16: Marvin King's Opel Station wagon
Source: Henry County Criminal Records Department

Relevant Facts and Dates

Figure 14
Serial Killer: The Casanova Killer, Paul John Knowles.
Source: Milledgeville Police Department

Sins of Henry County

Figure 15
Carl Isaacs and his gang of mass murderers
For those who don't know the difference between a loving father and a serial killer or a group of mass murderers, by their looks, please compare them to Jerry Banks.
*Source: Georgia State Prison
in Jackson Georgia*

Relevant Facts and Dates

THE TIME LINE:

November 7, 1974: (Thursday)

2:30 p.m. The time of the murders.
5 p.m. Jerry Banks found the bodies.
5:45 p.m. Andrew Lake Eberhardt called the police.
6:15 p.m. Detective Barnes and Sgt. Charles Tomlinson arrived.
Mid-evening: Andrew Lake Eberhardt met with Sheriff Jimmy Glass.
9:30 p.m. to 10:00 p.m. The bodies were removed from the crime scene and taken to Carmichael's Funeral Home.
11:00 p.m. The autopsies began by Dr. Howard from the GBI.
12:00 midnight. The Officers Barnes and Billy Payne picked Jerry up at his house and drove him to the Sheriff's Office to make a statement.

November 8, 1974: (Friday)

4:30 a.m. the Henry County police returned to the crime scene.
5:00 a.m. the Clayton County police arrived with a generator and lights to begin a search of the crime scene.
5:00 a.m. Jerry Banks was driven home but no one remembered who the officer was.
9:00 a.m. Lead Det. Phillip Howard and Det. Ted Ray found the first 2 shells.
November 9, 1974: (Saturday)
At some unknown time the first two shells which were found at the crime scene were sent to the GBI. They were 12-gauge Winchester Western 00 buck.
November 10, 1974: (Sunday)
Detective C.R. (Dick) Barnes went to Banks' house to pick up his Stevens shotgun.

Lead Det. Phillip Howard, Det. Dick Barnes and Det. Paul Robbins testified they test-fired Jerry Banks' shotgun behind the Henry County courthouse. There were three rounds fired. Lead Det. Phillip Howard testified he gave them to Sgt. Tommy Floyd.

December 2, 1974:

Lead Det. Phillip Howard sent his three test-fired shells to the GBI to compare with the two shells found at the crime scene on November 8, 1974. They were delivered by Officers Barnes and Robbins.

December 4, 1974:

The GBI ballistics expert, Kelly Fite called Sgt. Tommy Floyd informing him that the two shells found at the scene had been fired from Jerry Banks' shotgun.

December 5, 1974:

Det. Paul Robbins and Sgt. Floyd went to the home of Jerry Banks. They talked with him, read him his rights and asked him if they could borrow his shotgun again. They had to pick it up at Perry Banks' home and then they took Jerry Banks to their office for questioning.

December 6, 1974:

Det. Dick Barnes took the shotgun to the GBI so Kelly Fite could test-fire the shotgun himself. His findings were that they all matched those found at the murder site. They all came from the same gun, Jerry Banks' shotgun.

December 11, 1974:

Jerry Banks was arrested.

Relevant Facts and Dates

DECEMBER 12, 1974:

Detectives Paul Robbins and Bill Hart along with Sgt. Floyd took Jerry Banks back to the crime scene. It was then that Jerry told two different stories of how he found the wallet and pointed to where he tossed it.

BY THE GEORGIA SUPREME COURT:

"On December 12, 1974, appellant said he had loaned the gun to another person (Robert George, living on Mosley Road of Stockbridge) on the day of the murders. After the named person denied any knowledge of the incident, the appellant refuted his statement and said he had lied to "get the officers off his back."

DECEMBER 13, 1974:

A search party went back to the crime scene and Officer Bill Hart found the third shell and the wallet was found where Jerry had pointed the day before. The third shell was given to GBI at that time at the crime scene.
The court appointed Attorney A. J. Welch to represent Jerry Banks. I have no record of when John Hudson Myers was hired.

JANUARY 9, 1975:

The arraignment of Jerry Banks in Henry County.

JANUARY 28, 1975:

1st trial began and lasted two days.

JANUARY 31, 1975:

The jury returned a verdict of guilty and a death sentence.

February 4, 1975:

The motorist, Andrew Lake Eberhardt learned Jerry Banks had been found guilty and that the motorist that Banks claimed to have flagged down may not have ever existed and that Mr. Banks was going to die.

September 15, 1975:

After being denied a new trial by the trial judge, Judge Sosebee, the Georgia State Supreme Court reversed that denial based on new evidence. The missing motorist came forward.

November 17, 1975:

The second trial lasted two days. Jerry Banks was found guilty a second time. Jerry Banks was ordered to die in the electric chair in Georgia's State prison in Jackson.

1976:

Defense Attorney Hudson John Myers appealed to the U.S. Supreme Court for a new trial but disappeared after stopping by Mrs. Banks' home.

1977:

Attorney Alex Crumbley first talked to Jerry Banks and takes his case.

March 1978:

Attorney Alex Crumbley was appointed to the bench and he assisted in forming a new legal team.

Attorneys A. J. "Buddy" Welch, Wade M. Crumbley and Stephen P. Harrison formed the pro bono trio.

April 1978:

United States Supreme Court denied Banks' appeal for a new trial.

Summer of 1978:

The new team of lawyers filed a motion with local Judge Sam Whitmire for a new (third) trial based on Attorney John Hudson Myers' ineffective defense. Judge Whitmire denied this request.

November 1978:

The new team of lawyers appealed this to Georgia State Supreme Court and was denied again. (Also based on Hudson John Myers.)

Spring of 1980:

The private investigator, Doug Moss, proved the test-fire did not take place on November 10, a Sunday, but on the 8th a Friday. The trio of lawyers found the Jerry Banks case file with all the witnesses whose names had been withheld by the Sheriff's Office and they went to Judge Hugh D. Sosebee asking for a new trial based on new evidence. He was not affected by their findings and again denied Banks a new trial.

June 9, 1980:

Georgia Supreme Court granted a third trial again because of new evidence based on the witnesses who were withheld from the defense.

December 15, 1980:

District Attorney Bryan Smith announced he would try the case and deliver another death sentence against Jerry Banks.

December 16, 1980:

More new evidence from County Commissioner Buddy Kelley.

December 22, 1980:

Jerry Banks was reunited with his family before Christmas. Jerry Banks was a free man.

March 29, 1981:

The police report showed Jerry Banks killed Virginia and himself.

May 1981:

The new team of attorneys received an award.
December 18, 1981:
Nannie L. Dodson (Jerry's mother) filed a 12 million dollar suit against Jimmy Glass and his department on the behalf of Jerry's three children.

1981:

Jimmy Glass was arrested by the FBI on charges of importing drugs.

PART IV:
PRO BONO LAWYERS

CHAPTER 12

Answered Prayers

If you remember after my first trip to the courthouse when I finally got a look at the trial transcripts, I also called Jerry Banks Jr. shortly after.

We had a very pleasant conversation over the phone. I asked him if he had a problem with me writing a book about his father. He said he didn't and he was surprised that someone had not done it sooner. Our conversation ended much too early as I told him, "Jerry, I must end here. I have an appointment with one of your father's lawyers. The third one to be precise is Mr. Alex Crumbley. I really must run."

The last words I heard from Jerry Banks Jr. was "Please call me back and let's talk some more. I would love to hear what he has to say. Please call, okay."

I have no way of knowing why Jerry Banks Jr. never took another call from me, but I totally respect that.

✣ ✣ ✣

In order to keep this from being more confusing than it already is, allow me to direct you through the different time periods.

I will lead you through the time line. I will be telling you of my meeting with Attorney Alex Crumbley which took place around 2008.

1. Attorney Alex Crumbley will lead us back to 1976 and explain his time spent with this case and how he eventually handed it over to three other lawyers.
2. We will then cover their involvement from 1978 to 1981, what they discovered, how they discovered their evidence and how they used it.
3. We will then return to my meeting with Attorney Alex Crumbley where he will produce this evidence for me in 2008.

Meeting with Attorney Alex Crumbley:

Walking up to Attorney Alex Crumbley's office on Griffin Street, I was excited beyond control. Most of the streets entering McDonough Square are lined with beautiful Southern, stately white homes and surrounded by either oak or pecan trees.

And before we go any further, down here a "pee-con" is what we use to make pies and a "pee-can" is something our grandparents kept under the bed.

There couldn't have been more than one or two homes between his office and the small downtown area that makes up the town square. As I walked toward the front porch, the "builder" in me was amazed at the workmanship in this old home Attorney Alex Crumbley now calls his Law Office. Entering his office and standing in the foyer, I was warmly greeted by his secretary and directed to enter his office, which would have been the "Pa-lor." This would be the ell-shaped portion of the home that protrudes out toward the street.

The double-French doors were open and, as I stepped in, he rose to his feet as perfect Southern Gentlemen do, and a calm came over me as I knew there were no Sins that had come from this office. I introduced myself by my first name, Charles, and I knew at that moment, this was going to be my most memorable

Answered Prayers

and honored interview. I did ask him, "Is 'Your Honor', still appropriate?"

He laughed and said "I'll answer to almost anything."

Attorney Alex Crumbley was and is a fine and honorable man. He was a lawyer in 1976 when he first met Jerry Banks. In 1978 he became a judge in our fair town. He has now returned to his private law practice, and I would guess his age to be early sixties.

I was not going to waste his time with small talk so I started down my list. He relayed to me that he didn't know anything about Attorney Hudson Myers.

I told Attorney Crumbley that, in my mind, I thought he was the answer to Jerry's prayers.

"Well, I did rescue Jerry from the jail house," he said. He also said, "You know, I haven't given this trial much thought lately. It's been over 30 years."

I responded, "I haven't been able to forget it in 35 years."

"I started the public defender's program in a four-county area, here in the Flint District area. This was something new that had been started under the Nixon administration. I would go around from courthouse to courthouse representing the indigent."

"While at the Henry County Courthouse in 1976, I was told Jerry Banks wanted to see me. I knew who Jerry Banks was, I read the papers, and I did go over to talk to him through the bars, at the bullpen. Banks had not heard from his lawyer in some time. Banks also had heard they had lost the appeal (for the third trial) in the Supreme Court of Georgia and Myers was appealing that decision to the U.S. Supreme Court. But Banks had not heard from Myers and was worried."

After checking into Jerry's situation, Attorney Alex Crumbley took over Jerry's defense and started working on the appeals, which worked out to Jerry's advantage. Jerry's Attorney Hudson John Myers had disappeared. He had unexpectedly and quickly left town during the night.

"It was January of 1977. I remember because my wife and I went to Washington D.C. for President-Elect Jimmy Carter's inauguration. While there, I went to the U.S. Supreme Court House, walked in and introduced myself to the clerk. I had asked her to please see if she could check on the status of Banks v Georgia. Charles, she looked at me and said, 'Oh, Mr. Crumbley, there's no need to even look that up. Everybody up here knows about that case.'"

While Attorney Alex Crumbley was at the U.S. Supreme Court he found out Attorney Hudson John Myers had not filed a brief. He had just filed a poem!

What did this mean? I have no idea but it sounds like it was wrong.

Attorney Alex Crumbley returned to Atlanta and proceeded where Myers had failed. In the spring of 1977, the U.S. Supreme Court turned down the Banks appeal. Attorney Alex Crumbley continued on with his battle with the U.S. Supreme Court arguing that Jerry Banks deserved a new trial on grounds of ineffective council on the part of Attorney Hudson John Myers.

Hudson John Myers was later disbarred because this was not the first time he had failed a defendant in such a manner.

But I know any lawyer would have failed, if all things were equal.

Getting the Banks case back on track, of course, took time, years if not longer. During this time, the spring of 1978, Attorney Alex Crumbley was appointed to the bench in Henry County, which put him in the position of finding Jerry Banks a new attorney. He did even better; he went to his friends, Attorney A. J. "Buddy" Welch and Attorney Stephen P. Harrison and asked them to consider taking Jerry's case. They agreed to take the case pro bono. The third member of the dream team was Judge Alex Crumbley's younger brother Wade Crumbley, who was finishing up his law degree at the University of Georgia. He started right in helping his old childhood friend, Jerry Banks, as soon as he came home.

✠ ✠ ✠

Answered Prayers

BRIEF BACK STORY:

That's right ... Jerry and Perry Banks, Hardrock, and Wade Crumbley all grew up in Kelleytown, a small community a few miles north of the courthouse in McDonough. The main road leading into Kelleytown is called Crumbley Road. Perry and his life-long friend, who went by the name "Hardrock," (also a young black man) claimed to have taught Wade Crumbley how to catch his first bass.
In the South women catch brim and men catch bass.
Perry said, Hardrock carried Wade Crumbley on his bike everywhere they went. Perry told me, "Hardrock's grandparents and the Banks' grandparents and even their great grandparents picked cotton on the Crumbley's farm as far back you could remember." Perry Banks actually told me that Hardrock and Wade Crumbley were the closest to each other, growing up. I asked Perry one day what Hardrock's real name was. He told me but when I asked for the proper spelling, he laughed and said, "Hell, I don't know."
I laughed and said, "Me neither! We'll go with Hardrock. I don't think it would be wise to bother Judge Wade again with this."
They were worlds apart in some ways, but they were childhood friends as they grew up in this small Southern town. I guess one would refer to that as one of those full-circle events. Well here's another one for you. Remember the court-appointed attorney that the people in Atlanta advised Mrs. Banks to fire because they didn't think he would have Jerry's best interest at heart? Well that was Attorney A. J. "Buddy" Welch.

⚓ ⚓ ⚓

TRANSITION OF LAWYERS:

Everything that Defense Attorney Alex Crumbley had presented to the U. S. Supreme Court had been rejected.
In 1978, while Attorney Alex Crumbley was at the Henry County Courthouse to be sworn in as our new judge, a young lady

by the name of Cindy Glazier, a local newspaper reporter, came to him with information about the case. He kindly instructed her to see his younger brother, Wade Crumbley, about those matters.

Cindy Glazier then went directly to the new team of lawyers and shared with them a very troubling story. It turns out there was a witness from back on November 7, 1974, who had called Sheriff Jimmy Glass at his home to give him information about the murders, but no one ever called him back. He had heard Banks was on his way to death row and called Mrs. Glazier directly to give his story about the events of that day. This witness was Mr. Dean Floyd, and his statement was monumental. There was a pattern growing, first Andrew Eberhardt and now Dean Floyd. This witness statement was earth shattering but even more so when you consider that this information was smothered in order to gain a wrongful death sentence in two different trials of an innocent 23-year-old black man and to what avail. The wall of lies starts crumbling.

It is my thinking that Crumbley, Welch, and Harrison realized, with this kind of witness coming out of the woodwork over 4 years later, with stories like this, they needed help.

And then, too, there was a nagging question. If Sheriff Jimmy Glass had not been able to remember Andrew Lake Eberhardt's name and his statement, my Lord, how many more lost witnesses could be out there, walking the streets?

According to Mr. Dean Floyd, the Sheriff had Alzheimer's or his recorders were the sloppiest in the state.

Was someone not telling the complete truth?

1978, THREE YEARS AFTER THE SECOND TRIAL:

Jerry Banks had three new lawyers. I'll skip all the legal jargon and all the procedures that were about to take place. Believe me, it was a battle to the end. We have been through the evidence from the beginning up through the second trial and beyond. Keep in mind Banks was kept in the Henry County jail (the old bullpen) from December 11, 1974, until the end of his second trial which ended on November 18, 1975. After that, at some point in time he was sent to the Georgia State Prison in Jackson, Georgia, where he was on death row for at least three years or more.

Can you imagine the pain in his heart, the despair and the loneliness this man went through all those years? Jerry Banks would sit there on death row and his only hope was his new team of lawyers. But think about it, if you were going to die and you didn't have much of a chance of overcoming it, who else would you want but your childhood friend to fight for you? All those prayers over the last four years or so were starting to show results indeed.

Attorney Buddy Welch had been in his law office since 1970. Young Wade Crumbley, who was fresh out of the University of Georgia, may have been picked to do the foot work. They were all considered fairly young in their trade and found themselves taking on the biggest case in Henry County's history, even to this day.

There is a great story about how Attorney Buddy Welch suspected one of the police officers of suspecting others on the force of being involved in this frame job. As I understand it, Attorney Buddy Welch had a conversation with several police officers, letting out information (what we call today a "trial balloon"). It was said that Attorney Buddy Welch followed one officer home. As he watched behind the bushes, he observed this officer going downstairs to his basement. Mr. Welch entered the home and went down the stairs himself, overhearing a phone conversation with another detective, "You need to come clean on this thing. It's going to blow wide open!"

Then one day Welch, Crumbley, and Harrison received a call. It was a tip about one of the deputies who had left the department. It turned out when he left the department he took copies of the entire file on the Banks investigation!

I think this deputy knew the case was going to resurface and he wanted the goods on some people within the Sheriff's Department. Insurance, some may say. I also think he had to be afraid for his life. Now, just spitballing, again: how many people do you think would have known about this deputy and his file? Where do you think they worked? It is my guess that this tidbit of information came out of the Henry County Sheriff's Office.

I have already been out on a limb so I'll move a little further out and make a wild guess as to which officer had this file. I went back over piles of documents looking for an officer who would fill this bill. It had to be an officer around in the beginning, but who did not stay very long, an officer who knew enough of the daily activities that he would have been called to testify, even though he did not want to. Not like Officers Glover or Tomlinson, it needed to be someone in the loop.

As far as people like Jerry Banks and Detective Tommy Floyd, they were truthful; then, you learn to look for the one who answers in short, matter-of-fact statements. And it helped when this officer's name popped up on my list of people who I could not find. He would be someone who left the department, very, very quickly. There was only one officer who jumped out of the documents and slapped me between my eyes. It was during the second trial that Officer Bill Hart testified that he was with Henry County at the time of the murders but since had joined the Clayton Jr. College Police Department.

I believe it was Officer Bill Hart who took this file and he had good reason to take this information with him when he decided to no longer work for Sheriff Jimmy Glass.

Based on information given to me by Perry Banks in regard to the death of one of the deputies involved in his brother's arrest and conviction, I can only speculate as to why he held onto this file. He knew he also could be found lying under a red bedspread someday or lying dead on a lonely bridge.

With that said, I believe there were people involved, involuntarily. I'll bring you up to speed in time, but first things first.

Attorneys Welch, Crumbley, and Harrison located the deputy who I'll refer to as Bill Hart until proven otherwise. He agreed to turn over the file to Jerry's attorneys. Inside Bill Hart's file there were close to a dozen witnesses who had come forward with vital information that would have not only been helpful to Jerry Bank's defense but also would have proven that it was impossible for Jerry Banks to commit the murders. How about next to impossible? Ok, at least reasonable doubt, you be the judge. If you remember Mr. Dean Floyd, he was the witness who notified Cindy Glazier. His name and statement was in this hidden file along with many others.

This was not just new evidence; it was as exculpatory as it gets. Four years after the second trial had come and gone, while Jerry Banks was sitting on death row, the trio of lawyers brought this evidence before the local trial judge (which I will not name here) for a new trial and was turned down. I would like to think a judge of any kind would see this exculpatory evidence as a clear indication Jerry Banks did not receive a fair trial, but also it might be impossible for Jerry to have committed the murders. The meaning of exculpatory evidence is any evidence (in this case) discovered by the Prosecutor's Office or the Sheriff's Department that would be beneficial to the defendant (in this case Jerry Banks) but withheld (in this case covered up). How could this judge turn way from this new evidence and allow an innocent man to die?

If the truth had been known, any reasonable law enforcement agency with this type of witness statements would never have arrested Jerry Banks in the first place. There is no telling how high this goes.

I had only heard bits and pieces of this evidence over the years but it was never confirmed. It was never printed in the local paper or handed out for the public to read. This information was known only to the District Attorney's Office, the local and State Supreme Court and the Defense Attorneys.

Jerry Banks was to be given a third trial by the Georgia Supreme Court based on the evidence in Bill Hart's file and I had to learn what that evidence was. Without that, I wouldn't have a book and Jerry Banks would be just another criminal freed by a group of criminal lawyers.

✧ ✧ ✧

BACK TO MY MEETING WITH ATTORNEY ALEX CRUMBLEY:

During the close of one of my conversations with Jerry's third lawyer, retired Judge Alex Crumbley, he pointedly but kindly asked, "Why are you going to all this trouble? These people have been dead for over thirty years."

I explained, "This was something that had to be done." As I walked toward the door, concluding our meeting, I stopped, turned and I simply asked, "Do you know why Jerry Banks was given a third trial? You realize the evidence presented to the Georgia Supreme Court had to be substantial for things to have worked out the way they did."

Alex Crumbley looked at me and said, "No. I didn't handle Jerry's case for very long and I had no way of knowing if he killed those people or not. It was my job to see that he received a fair trial and then I became a judge and that was it."

As I thanked him for his time and I was turning to leave, he suddenly said "Wait a minute."

He returned to his desk and I to my chair. I believe he made a quick phone call while going to his computer and within a few minutes, while mumbling to himself, he said, "I believe I can find out pretty quick."

This took several minutes as I waited knowing this, along with the trial transcripts, would be a great way to begin my book.

He swiveled around in his chair with a look of interest, then leaned back in his chair as though he was about to unleash the whereabouts of Jimmy Hoffa. As he read out the litany of sins, I had to lean back in my seat. I could not believe what I was hearing.

"Well, you wanted to know. Here it is." He stood up and handed the print-out to me.

"Good luck with your book. I hope this will help."

I did not want to put this in my words as I felt sharing this document (the best I can in duplicating it) would allow you to see it, the same way I did.

268 S.E. 2d 630
246 Ga. 1, 268 S.E. 2d 630
(Cite as: 246 Ga. 1, 268 S.E.2d 630)

Supreme Court of Georgia
Banks
V.
The State
No. 36175
Argued May 13, 1980
Decided June 9, 1980
[*Note: The underlining of key words, by the Author*]

Defendant, who had been convicted on <u>circumstantial evidence</u> of murder, appealed from denial by the Henry Superior Court, Sosebee, J., of his extraordinary motion for new trial based on newly discovered evidence, The Supreme Court, Undercofler Chief Justice, held that newly discovered evidence presented by defendant entitled him to a new trial.

Reversed.

Bowles, J., dissented.
*1 UNDERCOFLER, Chief Justice.

This appeal involves an extraordinary motion for a new trial in the death case based on newly discovered evidence. The trial court denied the motion. We reverse.

Marvin King, a Jonesboro High bandleader, and Melanie Hartsfield, a former student, were found murdered in a wooded area of Henry County. The evidence showed that they were killed by two shotgun blasts each, one in the back and one in the head, from close range, at approximately 2:30 p.m. on November 7, 1974. Later that afternoon, Jerry Banks, while deer hunting with a dog, discovered the bodies and alerted the police by flagging down a passerby, who called the sheriff. When three red Winchester-Western 00 shotgun shells, found 30 to 50 feet from the murder site, were traced to Banks' gun, he was indicted and tried for the murders. Banks' gun was an old single-barrel 12-gauge shotgun.

Banks' first conviction and death sentence were reversed on a Brady v. Maryland error, because the sheriff had not revealed to the defense the passerby's name, although it was known to him. **Banks** v, **State**, 235 Ga.121, 218 S.E.2d 851 (1975). On retrial, **Banks**' subsequent conviction and death sentence were affirmed, **Banks** v. **State**, 237 Ga. 325, 227 S.E.2d 380 (1976). With three judges dissenting to the imposition of the death sentence. **Banks**' habeas, based inter alia on the ineffective assistance of his since disbarred attorney, was denied and affirmed on appeal. **Banks** v. Glass, 242 Ga. 518, 250 S.E.2d 431 (1978) (Hill, J., dissenting.) See Patrick v. **State**, 238 Ga. 497, 233 S.E.2d 757 (1977); Baily v. **State**, 139 Ga.App. 321, 228 S.E.2d 357 (1976)

At the hearing on this extraordinary motion for a new trial, **Banks** presented newly discovered evidence that meets the standards set out in Bell v. **State,** enlisting him to a new trial. Giving the circumstantial nature [FN1] of the case against him, we cannot say that the new evidence would not have resulted in a different verdict. This is especially true, where, as here, there is so much new evidence that real doubt is created that Banks has heretofore received a fair trial. The new evidence is summarized below.

> FN1. Code. Ann. S 38-109 provides: "to warrant a conviction on circumstantial evidence, the proved facts shall not only be consistent with the hypothesis of guilt, but shall exclude other reasonable hypothesis save that of the guilt of the accused."

1. <u>Four men</u> building a house about 800 yards from the murder site heard several shots fired in <u>rapid succession</u> at 2:30 the afternoon of the killings, November 7th, 1974. This information was related to two detectives doing a neighbourhood survey the next day. A memo was circulated among all the detectives, but <u>has since disappeared</u> from the files. All four men appeared (one by deposition) at the motion hearing and testified that the shots they all heard were inconsistent with a single-shot shotgun and came from the direction of the murders.

2. A farmer, (said to be <u>Dean Floyd</u>) outside building a calf pen, heard several rapid-fire shots at 2:30 p.m., from the direction in which the slayings occurred. Several minutes later, he passed near the murder site on the way to pick up his son at school, and noted a black van parked atop a bank by the road. A <u>white man</u> in an army jacket had his foot propped up on the back of the van, while smoking a cigarette and holding a shotgun that looked like a <u>Browning automatic</u>. After he heard about the murders the next day, this witness <u>called Sheriff Glass at home</u> about eight that night to pass along this information. <u>Sheriff Glass does not recall</u> the phone call.

3. Paul Collier, Sr., the Stockbridge Chief of Police, (Stockbridge is a city within Henry County) his son, also a policeman, and a game warden were at the city dump to test fire the warden's pistol. While they were setting up targets, the two policemen recall hearing three or four shots from a weapon fired in rapid succession, too fast to be from a single-shot gun, come from the direction of the killings. The warden was wearing earmuffs because of deafness caused by firing guns and did not hear any shots. The chief of police called the Sheriff's Department and related the information. No one there remembers taking such a call.

4. Another man, about noon on November 7th, 1974, recalled having seen two cars, one cream-colored Chevy he <u>took to be an unmarked police car</u> by its antenna, and the other, a dark-colored, small station wagon (the victim, King, was driving a red Opel station wagon) on a road about <u>a half mile</u> from the scene of the murders. A woman, sitting in the passenger side of the station wagon, was trying to pull the smaller of the two men back into that car. The two men were facing each other and <u>clearly arguing</u>. The witness went to the Henry County Sheriff's Office and <u>told this story to two detectives</u>, who made a written memorandum. Two detectives claim this memo is still in the file.

5. Mayor George Hart of Stockbridge, visiting the scene of the murders two days after the killings with Chief Collier, found two green shotgun shells in the grass a few feet off the roadbed from where the killings had taken place. He turned them over to Chief

Collier, who <u>notified Sheriff Glass's office</u>. Someone from that office picked up the shells that Collier had placed in an envelope several days later, but no one now recalls doing so and these <u>shells have disappeared</u>.
[The ballistics experts from the GBI were recalled to consider the above statements and to re-examine Jerry Banks' shotgun.]
6. The <u>ballistics experts</u> who testified said Banks' gun (a breaktop) <u>could not have fired in rapid succession</u>; that no less than four to five seconds would be necessary to break the gun, throw out the spent shell, reload and re-fire it. In addition was that the stock was loose, that <u>half the time, upon breaking the gun, it came apart,</u> and the ejector did not throw the empty shells out of the gun.

The ballistics experts also noted that the wounds were consistent with either an automatic or a single-shot weapon. Only one wound contained the white polyethylene packing granules unique to the Winchester Western 00 shell that were linked to Banks' gun. The experts testified that, at the close range from which the shots were inflected, they would have expected similar granules in or near the other wounds as well. [FN2] one expert added, however it was possible that the granules just did not stick in the wounds.

> FN2. The expert's testimony was that neither white granules, which are found only in Winchester-Western shells, nor black granules, which, among other brands, are contained in green Remington-Peters shells, were discovered in the other three wounds. Other brands of 12-gauge 00 shotgun shells do not contain any such granules.

Because we have concluded that this newly discovered evidence raises sufficient question about the verdict in **Jerry Banks'** earlier trial to warrant a retrial, we need not here reach the Brady, supra, issue regarding the newly discovered evidence.
In another enumeration, **Banks** raises as error the refusal of the trial court to make the prosecution's case file, which was inspected

in camera, a part of the record on appeal. It was, however, ordered sealed by the trial court pursuant to its inspection as a result of a new Brady motion filed by **Banks**. We ordered the file transmitted to this court and have made an in-camera review of it.

In his new Brady motion, Banks seeks to discover any other evidence, unknown to him, possessed by the **state**. Along with a general request for exculpatory evidence, **Banks** specifically requested other shells found at the scene and other persons noted in the area of the murders the afternoon of November 7, 1974. The **State's** file reveals a "**12-gauge S&W Fiocci cartridge** case identified as found at the scene" as well as statements by two passerby of other cars seen in the area that afternoon. We have by separate order designated these items for release to Banks, and have returned the sealed file to the trial court.

We make clear here that this order in no way precludes further action by the trial court regarding Banks' Brady motion in light of further evidence which may later develop. On the record now before us, we find no other evidence that must be released to Banks.

Judgment reversed.

All the Justices concur, except BOWLES, J., who dissents
Ga. 1980.
Banks v. state
246 Ga. 1, 268 S.E.2d 630
END OF DOCUMENT

⚓ ⚓ ⚓

You have seen the witnesses' statements, two of which were Paul Collier, Sr., the Stockbridge Chief of Police and his son. And they did not appear at the 1st or 2nd trial. These witnesses were never called and the names were withheld from the defense by someone in the Sheriff's Department. Again this kind of thing does not get swept under the rug in the Sheriff's Office, unless there are a whole lot of people doing a whole lot of sweeping.

There are people who say the Stockbridge Police Department was dismantled and the Sheriff's Department took over their duties. I have not had any luck contacting either of the Colliers but rumor has it they were run out of law enforcement in Henry County much the same way Attorney Hudson John Myers was taken out of the picture when drugs were found in his trunk.

Perry Banks told me, "Hudson John Myers was good at heart and he did the best he could. He was good to my mama and never took one penny from her."

Perry said to me, "Hudson Myers came by the house after the second trial one night sometime back in 1978. He told my Mama that they planted drugs in his car and then pulled him over. That man was so scared he didn't know what to do. He drove off that night and we nor Jerry, heard from him again."

CHAPTER 13

The December 22 Hearing

After my interview with Mr. Alex Crumbley, I continued on, more determined than ever to see this through, regardless of how foolish I may have been in the eyes of others.

The question presented numerous times to me by people in the legal community was "Why are you writing this book?" My first response was much like George Mallory's when asked why he wanted to climb Mt. Everest…"Because it's there!" But to be polite, I always followed up with "because somebody needs to."

Those in the legal community had access to documents and were privy to all that went on. They were actually surprised, as though I was wasting my time, because they still are under the impression that everyone knows all about Jerry Banks' dealings with the Henry County Sheriff's Department. In that case maybe someone could tell me who pulled the trigger on November 7, 1974.

※ ※ ※

Officer Bill Hart and Lead Detective Phillip Howard were the first to leave the department. I'm not sure of the date for Bill Hart. I'm guessing he parted ways with Sheriff Jimmy Glass and company soon after Jerry Banks was sentenced to die the first time.

Of course Lead Detective Phillip S. Howard left town during the first trial. From what I can tell he testified during the first trial but I don't know if he was on the payroll. He went to work as an investigator for the coroner in Clayton County.

The true loyalists were Detectives Paul Robbins, Dick Barnes, Ted Ray and Billy Payne. I have no record of the whereabouts of Ray and Barnes. Paul Robbins retired and still lives in McDonough. Officer Billy Payne turned up dead one night, lying on a bridge as an apparent hit-and-run victim. The cause of death was determined by the Henry County Sheriff's Department. Maybe Billy Payne wasn't really that much of a loyalist after all.

With the evidence found in Bill Hart's file, the State Supreme Court already had cleared the way for a third trial. But on December 16, 1980, the new District Attorney, Byron Smith, wasted no time and immediately announced his decision to retry the case anyway and to see to it that Jerry Banks was indeed put to death. He was sure the evidence found at the crime scene, the three shells, would hold up under any pressure.

This decision by District Attorney Byron Smith brought forth another motion filed by the defense which was held on December 22, 1980. The Henry County Courthouse was under reconstruction. To the best of my memory it was due to a fire. This hearing was held at one of the local fire stations.

All of the additional evidence from Bill Hart's file was presented to the Prosecutors and the Sheriff's Department on that day as well as other relevant pieces of evidence which were also withheld from the Defense team. And then there was their ace up their sleeve.

All Evidence below was presented during the 1980 Hearing:

[*Other than the Ace, all new evidence came from Bill Hart's file*]
The bulk of the evidence was the five statements presented to the Georgia Supreme Court by the four construction workers along with Mr. Dean Floyd, Paul Collier, Sr. and his son, Frank

The December 22 Hearing

Walker and Mayor George Hart of Stockbridge, none of which were ever heard by either jury.

Kelly Fite of the GBI had never heard about the four rapid-fire shotgun blasts at 2:30 p.m. the day of the murders. However, after Jerry's lawyers presented this evidence to the GBI, Kelly Fite's statement was in support of Jerry Banks' innocence.

"The ballistics expert [Kelly Fite] who testified said Banks' gun (a break-top) could not have fired in rapid succession; that no less than four to five seconds would be necessary to break the gun, throw out the spent shell, reload and re-fire it. In addition was that the stock was loose, that half the time, upon breaking the gun, it came apart, and the ejector did not throw the empty shells out of the gun."

⊕ ⊕ ⊕

I had read a statement about how Jerry's boots were taken and they were put in the corner of the trailer and left there. I originally thought I had read it in the trial testimony. After re-reading several times, I could never locate that statement.

One day I remembered I had read that testimony while at the court house in Jerry's records several years back. It was not from a trial but from the hearing filed in December of 1980. These records were on a transparent, tissue-type paper not suitable for running through a copier, so I remembered I taped my reading of these documents. This line of questioning was based on information from Bill Hart's file.

BY THE DEFENSE:

Q. Where were the footprints?
A. "There was also a set of shoe prints found at the murder site and at the location where Marvin King's car was found, both prints were similar."
Q. What were the measures taken to record these prints.

A. "Well, after checking both sites, we determined they were very similar, and Detective Phillip Howard instructed me to just draw a sketch of the prints on a piece of paper."

That was a statement from one the officers and he made reference to "Jerry Banks' boots were taken and placed in the corner of the office."

This would have been on the night Jerry was taken in at midnight, to give his witness statement. In the biggest murder investigation in the history of Henry County, Lead Detective Howard elected to record the murderer's footprint by sketching it on a piece of paper. Not one time did Jerry's boots or that sketch come up during either trial.

✣ ✣ ✣

Jerry Banks testified:

Jerry was asked if he remembered when his gun was returned. Jerry Banks stated during the 1980 hearing, they never returned the gun to him. This was a true statement. They returned it to Perry Banks but no one knows by whom or when. When they did come back to get the gun the second time as stated in court, on December 5, it was then ... somehow at Perry Banks' house. Perry himself today doesn't know about who, when or how, it got there.

While on the stand, Jerry Banks was asked if he remembered when they first picked up his shotgun. He stated "When they took me home after keeping me up all night at the Sheriff's Office the night of the murders, they took my shotgun at 5:00 a.m."

✣ ✣ ✣

It was finally revealed in Bill Hart's file during that questioning when the name of a witness by the name of Mamian Webster

The December 22 Hearing

was brought up. It is still a mystery if Mamian came forward before or after the first trial. But the fact Mamian Webster came forward with this statement was good news to the Banks family. This information had never been released until I informed Perry Banks. I told Perry Banks about Webster's coming forward to help Jerry. All these years he was wrong about Mamian Webster.

Mamian Webster stated he was hunting with Jerry Banks on November 7, 1974, from the hours of 1:00 p.m. until sometime after 4:00 p.m., when they found the bodies together. He was a witness who supported Jerry's original and only statement, that he (now they) had found the bodies. This shows us that Mamian Webster Jr. did come forward but never got past the Henry County Sheriff's Office. That's okay, the fact is Mamian Webster's statement was made and withheld, and it showed Jerry Banks did go hunting at 1:00 p.m. and maybe Jerry was working on Mrs. Slaughter's house that morning but more importantly they found the bodies.

Bill Hart testified at the second trial. He was already working for Clayton Junior College and he had Webster's statement in his files when he left. This still does not tell me if he came forward before or after the first trial. The important part of this, Jerry was present during this hearing. I know for Jerry to hear Mamian did come forward to help him had to make him very proud of his cousin. Perry Banks said "There is no telling what they said to Mamian Webster Jr. to scare him so bad that he never came around family again in over 35 years." To this day Mamian's whereabouts are unknown to the Banks family.

✧ ✧ ✧

Mr. Charles Hartsfield testified:

Miss Hartsfield's car was found some five miles away in a Stockbridge parking lot at the intersection of Highway 138 and Highway 42. The Sheriff's Office informed Mr. Charles

Hartsfield he could pick up his daughter's car and take it home. Mr. Hartsfield testified during this hearing on December 22, 1980.

BY THE DEFENSE:
- Q. When the Sheriff's Department informed you that you could pick up Melanie's car, would you tell us what happened?
- A. When I first tried to start her car, nothing happened as though the battery was dead. I raised the hood and noticed there was a wire disconnected. After reconnecting the wire, her car started right up.

What does this tell us? Did Jerry Banks tamper with Melanie's car (which was five miles away) before noon that day, knowing the first person she would call for help would be Marvin King? Was this Jerry's master plan to draw Marvin King across county lines so he could take his money out of his wallet and then execute the two of them?

Did Jerry Banks know she would call Marvin King? Somebody did ....

CHAPTER 14

The Ace

The way things worked out, long before the December 22, 1980, hearing, in fact before they went before the Georgia Supreme Court with Bill Hart's file, they already had their "ace" in the hole. Jerry's new lawyers felt they needed more than this hidden file. So they put their private investigator, Doug Moss, on the time clock and on the trail of Phillip Howard.

They needed to nail Phillip Howard and that is what they did. This would be the new lawyers' first chance in defending Jerry Banks and they wanted to be loaded for bear.

Attorney Buddy Welch told me, Bill Hart's file was a drop in the bucket compared to their ace. They knew the new District Attorney Byron Smith and they knew he would not easily fold his tent on this case. This case was too big; it was a career-maker. Jerry's lawyers held onto the even stronger evidence in case they needed to fight another round. This information was far more damaging evidence to Smith's office and to Henry County itself. This newer evidence should have caused more questions to be asked about why Jerry Banks was railroaded in the first place. Even the legalists in Washington D.C. were still tuned in for this outcome.

Well as it turned out Mr. Doug Moss was as good as they come.

As they say down in South Georgia around Vidalia, "The boy knows his onions."

His investigation took him on a visit to the courthouse where the test-firing took place. As luck would have it, he was asking questions around the courthouse when he happened to meet with the County Commissioner Bud Kelley. Detective Moss was thinking maybe someone in the courthouse may have heard these shotgun blasts back in the first week of November of 1974. The problem was it would be extraordinarily unusual for someone to be in the courthouse on Sunday. It was this conversation with Commissioner Kelley that proved to be the ace in the hole. Mr. Kelley stated he remembered hearing the three shots at the rear of the court house one day. After all, that was unusual. This was something that had never happened before or since.

It was Detective Howard and others' testimony that he fired Jerry Banks' shotgun into a pile of dirt on a Sunday, November the 10, 1974. The problem for Detective Phillip Howard was the courthouse was closed on Sunday. Commissioner Bud Kelley stated he heard the shots on the day the court house was open and he was there working. He informed the private detective "It was on Friday, the 8th." [The murders were on a Thursday, the 7th.] The Court House was closed on Saturday and Sunday, the 9th and the 10th. The only day Commissioner Bud Kelley could have heard the three reports would have to be Friday, the 8th.

The courthouse opened at 8:00 a.m. Lead Detective Howard found the first evidence shell at the scene "... somewhere between 7:30 and 9:00 a.m.". The crime scene was only a short drive up the road, 15 minutes with the lights flashing.

Bud Kelley could not have heard the three shots until at least 8:00 a.m., one hour before the finding of the first two shells at the crime scene. This was their ace.

I can't confirm this with Bud Kelley today because of his age and health. His memory is gone; however his wife recalls he did testify to these facts. Although she did not remember if he looked out of a window and saw Detective Howard, she confirmed he was there on Friday, November 8, 1974, and he did hear three shotgun blasts, and that was his testimony. This was confirmed to me by Attorney

Buddy Welch and Superior Court Judge Wade Crumbley. If this is true, it means a Law Enforcement Officer, Detective Howard, and several others within the Sheriff's Office lied under oath during two death penalty trials. It all depends on who you believe.

I guess before one could say Detectives Barnes, Paul Robbins, and Phillip Howard were not lying, you would have to assume Bud Kelley was lying. If Bud Kelly was lying then so were three of the finest lawyers to ever take the oath. There is only one way to find out.

We all know now that just about everybody in this book grew up together in the little town of Kelleytown, named after the Kelleys. Bud Kelley did not however grow up with all of these fine young men, but he was there overseeing them.

The Kelley's were like many of the others. They all came from founding families of Henry County when it was created on May 21, 1821. Henry County is referred to in the book <u>The Mother of Counties</u> as being the largest county in the State of Georgia. Today there are seven counties bordering our county, all of which, at one time, were a part of Henry County. The history is strong and the good far ... far outweighs the "Sins" I have uncovered here.

I asked Buddy and Beau, Bud Kelley's son, and grandson if they had heard of Bud Kelley's involvement in this unbelievable case of State v Banks. They had not. I believe that Bud Kelley may not have known the importance of this testimony. It is my guess that his statement may have been given during a deposition while Jerry sat on death row down at Jackson State Prison. It was this testimony that freed Jerry Banks and saved his life.

✣ ✣ ✣

BACK TO THE ACE:

Meanwhile, all of the witnesses and their statements, once withheld, were of no concern to District Attorney Byron Smith. He was hell bent on going to trial again.

Earlier that year, Jerry's lawyers knew they needed to totally expose Det. Howard once and for all. They would need to find him and nail him to the wall so they could totally discredit him. This took even more money for P.I. Moss to put his ear to the ground but these lawyers pitched in. Attorneys Welch, Crumbley, and Harrison had already volunteered their services in Jerry's behalf. Had they been court-appointed, well things would have been different ... they might have been paid by the State of Georgia a little more than other Southern states, which only paid one thousand dollars.

Private Detective Doug Moss located Phillip Howard working for Georgia Power in South Georgia. The three lawyers hit the road running and nailed Howard's hide to the wall like a centerfold. They say they kept him up all night and ran him through the ringer. By the time these lawyers finished with Howard, his credibility as a witness in court was zero.

⚜ ⚜ ⚜

Jerry's three defense lawyers had done their job and planned to continue living and hopefully working in Henry County. But I do not think this matter had been put to rest with them. Bits and pieces of Mr. Moss's findings were released here and there over the years. The one thing that has never been released, to my knowledge in print or an open statement, was the details surrounding and describing their ace. I explained to Attorney Buddy Welch and Judge Wade Crumbley in 2010 that, in writing this book, I needed to know if it was true, for a fact, that Lead Detective Phillip Howard planted the shotgun shell evidence. They not only confirmed that fact but they both separately went on to explain how Lead Detective Howard pulled it off. I'll get to that later. This means their ace ... was ... there was never a "so-called" test-firing outside of the trailer behind the courthouse on that Sunday, November 10, 1974. The only problem is they could not prove it.

However, when their ace piece of evidence was shown to D. A. Byron Smith, he wasted no time dropping all charges. Although

The Ace

he did not exactly call the television station or the Atlanta papers about this embarrassment, his office did release a statement in which they took the credit for discovering this new information and bringing this case to an end!

⊕ ⊕ ⊕

After learning of all this extraordinary information, I placed another call to Mr. Dale Russell at Fox 5 in Atlanta. If you remember he said …"You need absolute proof that this young man did not commit the murders…You need proof that he was framed." I explained to him, I could do just that. He wasn't impressed but he did tell me to get back in touch with him when I finished the book. After a few years, as the book was nearing its end, I got tired of calling the station and leaving messages. Some things never change.

CHAPTER 15

Exculpatory Evidence

At one point, the Sheriff's Department was charged by the defense for not looking else-where for possible suspects. There was an individual who the Sheriff's Department was aware of but failed to pass this information to the defense. Could this individual have been responsible for the murders? Absolutely; he could have not only murdered the victims but this guy would have had a picnic on the red bedspread before leaving.

There is a great article in the Middle Georgia Magazine, "My Occupation: Serial Killer" by Wayne Dobson that I actually purchased in October of 2011 in Juliette, Georgia.

It starts out with Paul Knowles, **See Figure 14: Serial Killer: The Casanova Killer, Paul John Knowles,** purchasing a cassette tape recorder in Macon, Georgia, at a Zayre's department store using Mr. Carswell Carr's credit card. Macon and Milledgeville, where Mr. Carr and his daughter were slain, are very close together, so the news of the murders traveled fast. Police were given a description of a man matching a suspect in another murder of a hitcher Edward Hilliard and friend Debbie Griffen on November 2, 1974, also in the same area.

Paul Knowles began his violent spree after serving time in prison for crimes of theft. He, like many criminals, met a woman while in prison and planned to marry, but after his release she changed her mind. This angry young man reacted like a machine with its wires crossed. On July 26, 1974 in Jacksonville, Florida, he stabbed a bartender in a bar-room fight. Paul Knowles was arrested but escaped and then killed his first recorded victim, Alice Curtis. The police knew Paul Knowles was their suspect and his face was all over the news. Before he could leave town, while preparing to ditch Alice Curtis' car, he recognized two girls, eleven and seven-year-old sisters who knew his mother. To be on the safe side he murdered both girls and discarded their little bodies in the Florida swamp as he left them in his wake. He then murdered Marjorie Howe as he passed through Atlantic Beach because he needed her television in order to keep abreast of police and news reports.

His fifth victim was an unnamed drifter. She was raped and strangled. By August 23, 1974, Paul Knowles had worked his way into Musella, Georgia, near Milledgeville, where he murdered his sixth victim, Kathy Pierce.

Paul Knowles' seventh victim was William Bates in Lima, Ohio, on September 3, 1974. Knowles swapped Alice Curtis' car for William Bates' car. Emmett and Lois Johnson were murder victims eight and nine on Sept 18, 1974, while camping in Ely, Nevada. Paul Knowles raped and murdered Charlynn Hicks in Sequin, Texas. Knowles spotted her while working east across the country. Her motorcycle broke down which brought about her death. He raped and strangled her on September 21, 1974. When found, her body had been dragged through barbed wire.

As Paul Knowles passed through Alabama on September 23, 1974, he met and traveled with Ann Dawson from Birmingham, until his urge to kill overpowered his urge for pleasure. She was murdered on September 29, 1974. The location of her body is unknown.

His next two victims were Karen Wine and her 16-year-old daughter. On October 19, 1974, Doris Hovey from Virginia was murdered with her husband's rifle.

While still driving a stolen car of a dead man, Williams Bates, Paul Knowles was pulled over in Florida by police with his next two hitchhiking victims still aboard. With only a warning he was sent on his way to come to Georgia to continue his spree of death. After this close encounter, Knowles allowed the hitchhikers a pass.

Paul John Knowles seemed to have a connection with Georgia, or was it hatred. He was back again and before it would be over, five of his victims would be murdered in Georgia. Sadly enough his last four would be his most brutal. This may be because he had called and met with his lawyer, Sheldon Yavitz, who advised Paul Knowles to turn himself in. Paul Knowles gave his lawyer his taped confession and headed to Milledgeville, Georgia.

During the early morning hours of November 7, with 18 known murders to his credit, this serial killer, only a 40-minute drive south to Milledgeville from McDonough, just savagely murdered two of his 35 claimed victims, Mr. Carswell Carr and his young teenage daughter.

Paul Knowles was more than likely still driving a dead man's car, carrying another dead man's credit card and carrying another tape recorder with Lord knows what on it! And this was when he was questioned at a nearby hotel a few miles from where the Hartsfield/King murders took place. Yes, he was questioned by the Henry County Sheriff's Department on the day of the slaying, November 7. While talking to Henry County officers his heart was probably still racing from the adrenaline rush from what he had done to that poor young girl and the 20 plus stabbings of Mr. Carswell Carr, just hours earlier in Milledgeville. I have never been able to learn what prompted them to question him in the first place. It couldn't have been because he was on the FBI's most wanted list, so what was it?

Wayne Dobson's article made reference to Sandy Fawkes, a British journalist, who met Paul John Knowles in a bar in Atlanta the next night, November 8, 1974, and spent the night with him. Wayne Dobson quotes Sandy Fawkes from her book, <u>The Killing Time</u>. She writes "Knowles must have spent the day I met him recording the Carr murders on the machine he had bought at Zayre on Mr. Carswell Carr's credit card."

What I do know is Paul Knowles drove away from that hotel in Stockbridge, Georgia, only 10 days before his killing spree ended on November 18, 1974, right back in Stockbridge. The exact date is unknown but shortly after being released by Sheriff Glass's deputies, Paul Knowles murdered Mr. James Myers and Florida's State Trooper Charles Eugene Campbell. Trooper Charles Campbell had stopped Paul Knowles during a routine traffic stop in Perry, Florida. Campbell was overpowered by Paul Knowles and then he later abducted James Myers who was a businessman. While driving through Florida back to Georgia, he knew the end was near. He did not want to spend the rest of his life in prison. He wanted to die either in a gun fight or in the electric chair. He did not want to return to prison for life. He had carefully selected states during his spree which allowed the death penalty. Either way it was going to be over. This is why he stepped up the brutality and this was his connection with Georgia.

Paul Knowles knew they were waiting for him. I knew they were waiting for him. It was all over the news for days. Paul Knowles drove to Kathleen, Georgia, outside of Warner Robins and Perry. He forced Campbell and Myers into the woods near the Pabst Blue Ribbon brewery and handcuffed the two men to a tree, then murdered both of them with the trooper's gun.

Paul Knowles headed north toward Atlanta on I-75. This event was well-covered on the radio and television. He knew it would soon be over. It was at Stockbridge the task-force chose to set up their road blocks. This would be the last stop to keep Paul Knowles out of Atlanta. If they could not stop him there, we were all in trouble.

I have read stories where Paul Knowles and a police officer were both wounded in a final shoot out in Pulaski County, Georgia. There are stories where it all ended in Alabama but the killing spree ended with a gun-battle and manhunt in Henry County, Georgia.

On November 18, 1974, Paul Knowles tried to run through the road block, lost control of the car and crashed. It was said that he fired into the air to keep everyone back, but Officer Bill Hart drew fire from this notorious serial killer as he moved in. Paul Knowles ran into the woods where he was chased by dogs

Exculpatory Evidence

and a helicopter and soon after he was apprehended. Paul John Knowles was arrested and he happened to have a 12-gauge shotgun and 00 buckshot shells in his possession, matching the unique type used in the King and Hartsfield murders.

Now this is interesting but not the place for me to explain. I'll note my point at the end of this story.

Paul Knowles was transported for safe keeping to Douglasville, Georgia, some 40 miles west of Atlanta. Sheriff Earl Lee of Douglassville was at the top of the list of men up to the task of handling the likes of Knowles. Sheriff Earl Lee was the person responsible for housing and later transporting Paul Knowles to Atlanta to answer to charges in a string of murders up and down Interstate 75 from Georgia to Florida. I have also been told the reason for this trip was to return him to Stockbridge, so Paul Knowles could show them where he had tossed the murder weapon, Trooper Campbell's revolver.

The day I heard on the evening news that Paul Knowles was killed while trying to escape, my first reaction was ... they pulled over on Interstate 20, pulled Paul Knowles from the car, shoved him down an embankment and shot him.

I had the pleasure of having lunch with one of the Georgia State Patrol officers who answered that call when it came over the radio.

"No, no, nothing like that happened, I was there."

On the morning Paul Knowles was to be moved to Atlanta, six officers went in to Paul Knowles' cell to handcuff him. One or two officers would have been killed. Paul Knowles was a dangerous animal. He was big and mean and, with his martial arts skills, he was deadly and he enjoyed killing. This is one reason the State chose Sheriff Earl Lee to handle this notorious killer. Sheriff Earl Lee was and still is a legend in the state of Georgia. The State Patrol officer went on saying that on I-20, as they headed east to Atlanta, Earl Lee was driving and GBI Agent Ron Angel was in the front passenger seat, with Paul Knowles in the back seat with handcuffs and possibly foot irons. Somehow Paul Knowles produced a paper clip from his mouth and freed his hands. Paul Knowles carefully reached over the front seat grabbing Earl Lee's hand gun. This was before the days of metal shielding being used to prevent this from happening. Earl Lee yelled out while trying to prevent Paul Knowles from getting his gun out of his holster. One round went off in the scuffle. They were fighting over the gun and Paul Knowles was winning, because he had the advantage by his strength and position, in that he was pulling back on the gun.

"*He's got my gun. Oh my god, he's got my gun.*"

Ron Angel didn't blink an eye. He removed his revolver and shot over the front seat several rounds killing Paul John Knowles right there in the back seat of the patrol car alongside Interstate 20 East.

⚓ ⚓ ⚓

How did Henry County not know anything about Paul Knowles on November 7, 1974? The whole world was looking for him. He was driving a dead man's car. In 1980, during the extraordinary motion, Banks' three new attorneys felt this was exculpatory evidence that was withheld from the defense. It was something the defense should have been informed about during the first trial. If any jury knew Paul John Knowles was found a few miles from Rock Quarry Road on the day of the murders, it could have been shown that there were others out there more capable of this murder than Jerry Banks. The local trial judge disagreed.

⚓ ⚓ ⚓

Note: *A notorious serial killer was apprehended who had been stopped and questioned the day of the murder in Stockbridge and had in his possession a 12-gauge shotgun and shells matching the unique type used in the King and Hartsfield murders but it wasn't the Winchester Western brand. Paul Knowles had a type of 00 buck ammunition known as Fiocci.*

Exculpatory Evidence

Attorney A.J. "Buddy" Welch informed me the GBI was wrong when they stated in court that the white polyethylene packing granules were unique to the Winchester Western 00 brand. The manufacturer, Fiocci [a foreign brand] also used the same packing.

See Chapter 12. The Georgia State Supreme Court ruling reversing the decision of the first trial:

Banks specifically requested other shells found at the scene and other persons noted in the area of the murders the afternoon of November 7, 1974. The **State's** file reveals a "**12-gauge S&W Fiocci cartridge** case identified as found at the scene" ...

All I can say about this is somebody blew a chance of a life time when they let Paul John Knowles slip away. He was in Stockbridge the day of the murders. He was a serial killer. He had a 12-gauge shotgun with the right ammunition and he had just killed 18 other people. But believe me, he did not kill Marvin King and Melanie Hartsfield and neither did Jerry Banks.

I can only think of two reasons Paul John Knowles was not framed for the murders. Number one: Because there is an unwritten rule that you can only frame one person per crime. And number two: Jerry was chosen first and it was too late to ask the GBI for those evidence shells back.

CHAPTER 16

Clayton County Detectives

I have had many conversations with the Clayton County detectives. Retired Detective Keith Martin and now a lawyer, himself, informed me there was a Superior Court Judge in Clayton County willing to testify during the hearing on December 22, 1980, that he would not believe one word of testimony that came out of Phillip S. Howard's mouth. Phillip Howard had been caught in Clayton County mishandling shell evidence while he worked for the city police of Morrow.

Retired Detective Keith Martin described their investigation following the murders, on their side of the county line, as being vast. In those days the Clayton County detectives were working hard looking into any possible motives, like a jealous husband, wives, or boyfriends, anyone who might have a reason to kill two of their citizens. They found nothing.

I think it was possible Detective Howard waited until December 2 before forwarding the second set of test-fired shells to the Crime Laboratory because he was waiting to see if Clayton County had found any evidence of "the real killer" before he sent them to the GBI Crime Lab. It would have been more than embarrassing if Phillip Howard had sent the shells to Atlanta one day and the Clayton County police made an arrest of a suspect the next. Especially if their suspect wore a military jacket, drove a black van and had a Browning automatic 12-gauge shotgun. (See witness statement in Chapter 12.)

Mr. Keith Martin told me that finger printing and polygraph examinations were all Clayton County was providing on the front-end of the investigation. Thinking back 40 years, he recalled Jerry and/or Perry Banks may have been given a polygraph.

He said "It has been so long, but ... I'm not sure ... if Perry took one or not. It seems to me that Jerry was given the polygraph but he implicated Perry."

"How would that have been possible?" I asked.

"Well it would have been by inference, by a SKY question from the examiner. The best I remember he showed deception on a SKY question."

"What is a SKY question?"

"A SKY question is when they ask a "Do you know ... Do you have knowledge of ... Do you or anyone else ... type question? It seems to me, I remember this deception implicated Perry Banks. I can't be positive but I think they thought Perry was the killer and Jerry was covering for him."

I asked, "When you say a SKY question, could that have been stated. "Did you kill Marvin King and Melanie Hartsfield? And then ask, do you have any knowledge of anyone at the murder scene that day ... or something along those lines ... because he was not alone when he found the bodies. It's a long story, but he was there with his cousin, who didn't want to get involved ... so on and so on. If Jerry was covering for his cousin in the back of his mind and answered "No" to the SKY question, would that have rendered a deceptive response?"

"Oh, yes. They knew Jerry was not truthful, so it may have been a question involving or pertaining to someone else. They thought of Perry Banks and figured he was involved."

✧ ✧ ✧

I remember asking if the phone records of Marvin King and Miss Hartsfield were checked in November 1974. "Yes, we had the records of Mr. King and Melanie's parents checked and came up with nothing."

I checked with AT&T into the possibility that there would still be access to phone records for the year 1974. The phone records of Marvin King would help. I was told "Yes, we can pull up records that far back even on the phone in (Marvin King's office) the high-school band room, but it would take a court order."

"A court order," I repeated. "What would it take to get a court order?" I asked.

"Well you would get one from a judge but only if there was a new investigation."

I always thought the people who Marvin was involved with would have been calling the phone in his office, not his home phone. Marvin King was into too much for him to conduct his activities at home. His wife was totally in the dark. I don't think this murder just happened at the drop of a hat. Something was going on in King's life that came to a boil. I know these records would be the key to putting the final pieces together in this puzzle. Even if the people involved in setting up King had not made contact with threats over the phone, those records would tell stories of his associates.

⚜ ⚜ ⚜

My interviews on the Clayton County side of the line were not a complete loss. Because I do not wish at this time to enter into a possible libel area, I will not be able to go into a great deal of detail about something very interesting that was uncovered in Jonesboro, Georgia.

There has been one common theme which I have been made privy to over the last 30 plus years about a secret, underground lifestyle. The Clayton County police found nothing on Marvin King. Marvin King is not the villain here, and I'm not going to elaborate, but I will say he was not found to be breaking the law and there has never been anything linked to him that would indicate he was.

It is my thinking that Marvin King crossed this group of people. All I can think of is the known man Marvin King was fighting with in the summer of 1974, who was out of town when they were killed. Just because he was out of town doesn't mean anything.

PART V:
A TIME TO DIE

CHAPTER 17

Does Our System Work?

Perry Banks asked me if I could imagine what it must have been like for a young man to be falsely accused of murder and have to sit on death row for six years. Imagine what Jerry Banks went through every time he heard those footsteps and those keys jingling as they came down that hall, knowing someday soon they were coming for him. That was a serious place to be and in the company of the most notorious murderers in the history of Georgia, some of the worst in the history of this country.

Carl Isaacs and his gang murdered an entire family in such a cold-blooded manner on May 14, 1973, that it changed the way the people of Georgia went about their daily lives. **See Figure15: Carl Isaacs and his gang of mass murderers.** It was so severe that I, a grown man, had nightmares where I would wake up in a cold sweat, thinking my heart was going to jump out of my chest. In my nightmare, I was fighting Carl Isaacs at my bedroom window, trying to keep him away from my two babies and my wife. I could not stop these nightmares, and I could not stop this murdering animal from invading my fears. As I could not stop him, the fear overwhelmed me so much my mind stopped the dream, awakening me before my heart stopped beating. It wasn't until I asked for God's help that the fear and the dreams went away. I prayed that God would place a protective shield over my house to keep Carl Isaacs away from my family.

This is the sugar-coated version. If you could read the Atlanta Journal's write-up, you would better understand my nightmares.

(Sources: Associated Press & Rick Halperin) In May of 1973, Carl Isaacs escaped from a Maryland penal institution and, accompanied by his younger brother Billy Isaacs, his half-brother Wayne Coleman and a friend, George Dungee, they were passing through South Georgia on their way to Florida. They saw a gas pump behind the rural mobile home belonging to Jerry and Mary Alday and stopped to investigate.

Jerry Alday and his father Ned Alday pulled in behind the trailer, unaware that it was being burglarized. They entered the trailer expecting nothing. It was lunch time and others were on their way shortly behind. They were met by this ruthless gang and forced at gun point to one end of the trailer and into one of the bedrooms. They were ordered to lie down on the bed. Carl Isaacs shot and killed Jerry Alday with a shotgun, and then both he and Coleman (also firing a shotgun) shot and killed Ned Alday. Both men were found embracing each other on the bed.

Jerry Alday's brother, Jimmy, drove up on a tractor and was also forced inside at gunpoint, then was shot by Carl Isaacs. Jerry Alday's wife Mary Alday then drove up, then Chester and Aubrey Alday (Jerry's brother and uncle) drove up in a pickup truck. All three were forced inside. Aubrey was taken to the south bedroom where Carl Isaacs shot and killed him, while Chester Alday was taken to the north bedroom and killed by Coleman. As for Mary Alday's last two days on this earth, there is nothing I wish to write about. I had seen violence in movies long before the Alday massacre and even worse since then. But to tell you the honest truth, I was not aware there were sub-humans, like those animals walking the earth.

Around the late 80s there was a prison-break from Jackson Prison, where four or five prisoners escaped. The next morning the entire prison was inspected cell by cell. Inside Carl Isaacs's cell was found a makeshift prison uniform.

If you ever pass through Pennsylvania, look out for younger brother Billy Isaacs. He testified against his brother and the others in exchange for a plea agreement calling for a 40-year sentence. This individual was paroled early in 1994.

Carl Isaacs was the longest-serving inmate on death row in any state in the U.S.

I would truly say it was pathetic enough Carl Isaacs even occupied a soul. It sickened the people of Georgia when our laws allowed him to live on taxpayer dollars for 30 years after slaughtering six members of the Alday family. The appeals process which allowed this kind of thing to go on was talked about around Georgia for even more than the 30 years Carl Isaacs was allowed to live. Let me share with you something that will put this into perspective.

Faye Alday Barber, the daughter of Ned Alday, said there was something wrong with a legal system which allowed the people responsible for the Alday murders, Carl Isaacs and his gang, the worst mass murders in the history of Georgia, to go on for 30 years before bringing Carl to justice. Carl Isaacs was finally executed on May 6, 2003, in Georgia's State Prison in Jackson, Georgia, just 20 miles south of McDonough.

Mrs. Barber wrote, "We lost our family, our farms, and our heritage. We lost hope... but liberty was not lost; it was stolen."

She said the family dog, Tub, saw the bodies removed from the crime scene and never got over it.

"He went out into the field and laid down, refused to eat or sleep, wouldn't let anyone touch him, and over a period of time, his hair fell out, exposing rib bones that protruded through his skin. He was a pitiful sight. He became so thin that when it rained, he could have crawled under a honeysuckle vine to keep from getting wet. A veterinarian said (Tub) grieved himself to death. That dog had more compassion for my family than our courts."

That one statement is so powerful and so moving, even to this day. There is nothing in this world I would do or say to disagree with those words. To this day, I keep Mrs. Barber's words in my office, so I can read them from time to time. You see, the Alday family has also been in my mind and heart for over 35 years and they always will.

But here lies the rub. If it were not for this process of appeals that lasted so many years for Carl Isaacs, Jerry Banks surely would have been put to death in Georgia's electric chair and Attorneys Buddy Welch, Wade Crumbley, and Stephen P. Harrison would have never exposed Jimmy Glass, Dick Barnes, Phillip S. Howard, and Paul Robbins for what they did or did not do.

The political views were quite worrisome in those days, as well. This is a quote from a newspaper.

"This is not a perfect system. Yes, you are going to have mistakes. But, with any system, that's possible and (the execution of an innocent person) is an acceptable risk," said former Georgia Attorney General Michael Bowers, who was running for governor at that time.

CHAPTER 18

Jerry Banks' Journey Ends

In 1980, Jerry Banks had been in jail or prison for over six years, three on Death Row. There were times Jerry and his family felt this nightmare would never end, or, if it did, it would be by his death. Sadly enough, they were right. At this time though, according to the lawyers, things were capable of producing favorable results. But Jerry had heard those words before.

As for the public, the last thing they had heard was Jerry had been found guilty a second time and had been sent to Jackson State Prison. After that, there wasn't any news on the television or in the press about the case. Since the second trial, all the work was done behind closed doors. Sitting there on death row was distressing enough, but a few years earlier, the State of Georgia had brought back the electric chair. Those at the helm of the prison system had a load of people who they wanted to get rid of, who had been taking up space. Jerry Banks had been on that list for six years.

✥ ✥ ✥

Let's finish Jerry Bank's journey. Jerry Banks Sr.'s story is about to come to an end here. Jerry Banks had been transferred from the prison back to the bullpen in 1980 after he was awarded the third trial.

After the hearing on December 22, 1980, Attorney Wade Crumbley stopped by the jail and told Jerry there was not going to be a third trial and he was going home for Christmas. After six years, Jerry Banks was a free man. It was finally over. His childhood friend dropped Jerry off at his house. Virginia and the kids were still living in the same house on Banks Road. Jerry walked in on December 22 and it was like something out of the movies. His wife Virginia, Perry, his mother and his children were all totally surprised to see him walk through that door.

Adjusting to life on the outside proved to be difficult at times. Jerry did manage to get a job, thanks to some terrifically understanding people, and Attorney Wade Crumbley purchased him a car. However, things had changed between Virginia and Jerry. Because he was gone for so long and she had been living with the understanding that he would be put to death, she had moved on with her life and things were not ever going to be the same again between them.

While Jerry was away, his sister Mary-Joe was struck with multiple sclerosis. She took a fall and never walked again. She was bedridden for the last six years, until her illness took her life while Jerry was in prison. Everyone had given up on Jerry's chances. He was as good as dead, so Charles Crumbley, Mary-Joe's husband, and Jerry's wife found comfort with each other. Virginia had filed for a divorce. Jerry could not bear to lose her and his children, not after what he had been through.

On Sunday March 29, 1981, Jerry's brother Ludie's birthday, Jerry felt his entire world had finally come to an end. The story was he wanted to plead with Virginia one last time, not to go through with the divorce. It was to be final in three days.

Detective Tomlinson, off duty, drove up while Jerry was out in the front yard. Mr. Tomlinson was a virtuous Christian man with a ministry in which he helped others. He stopped by to check in on Jerry that day to see how he was doing.

I believe God put him there that day in hopes Jerry would reach out in some way.

You can only push a man so far, once you have taken everything a man's got, even his will to live. There's no turning back. You can't unscramble eggs. Jerry Banks gave Detective Tomlinson no indication there was anything wrong.

Shortly after Tomlinson pulled out and went on his way, Virginia returned home. Jerry Banks made a last plea with Virginia to work things out, but she had been pushed too far herself. She had been expecting Jerry to die for the last six years. Her hopes were long gone and Jerry getting off death row could not restore the past.

As Jerry Banks realized that this was the end of his journey, he took out a pistol. Virginia knew this wasn't going to turn out good.

As Virginia tried to run out of the house, Jerry Banks shot her. Then he put the gun to his chest and pulled the trigger.

"They had taken all that I had; all that I held dear to me." That was Jerry Banks' last written words.

They had totally destroyed an entire family. He had nothing to live for. Jerry did not understand all this himself. How can a man hold up under the pressure of knowing he's going to die in the electric chair for something he didn't do, for all those years but not be able to hold it together when he loses his family?

It's all over for Jerry. As far as his life flashing before him, he might have remembered those words that Mamian told him. "Jerry, let's get out of here. They are going to put this on you."

I feel in my heart that Jerry cried out to God again that day.

Jerry Banks was dead when he hit the floor. Virginia made it next door to her aunt's doorstep, but the damage was done. She collapsed there and never regained consciousness.

Within an hour Attorney Wade Crumbley, Perry Banks, and others arrived at what was now a new crime scene, but it was over. The police had the street blocked off and Perry was not allowed to go to his own brother or to be with Virginia. Virginia died over a month later.

I am sure Jerry Banks has been in Judge Wade Crumbley's thoughts over these years most likely more than mine. Judge

Wade Crumbley has been particularly protective of Jerry and Virginia's memory over the years.

Detective Tomlinson was more than likely the last person to talk to Jerry and Virginia just before their death. Tomlinson said, "I was in Atlanta that day with a friend and, on my way home, I thought I would stop and check on Jerry."

I asked, "Were you on duty?"

"No it was ... I think it was on a Saturday or Sunday. I'm not sure but it seems that's right. Jerry seemed alright at the time. I could not tell that anything was wrong."

Unaware of what was going on in Jerry's head, Tomlinson said his goodbyes and then he drove off. Down the road, he saw Virginia returning home and stopped to have a word with her.

He heard nothing out of the ordinary. Detective Tomlinson drove straight home, and when he walked through the door, his wife had already received a call that Jerry had just shot Virginia and killed himself.

Perry said, "Jerry had been calling everywhere looking for me and Hardrock that day. I had a feeling he was in trouble but I never found out what it was he wanted."

Virginia's parents were related to the Lemon family, one of the oldest families in Henry County, which owned Lemon Funeral Home. The Lemons put Jerry to rest at Bentley Hill United Methodist Church on Hwy 155 just north of McDonough and later, when Virginia passed, they placed her next to Jerry.

For the record, my record, I am telling the events of that day as they were relayed to me by several people involved. Primarily retired Detective Tomlinson was the only person said to be there. But he wasn't there; he drove off and went home. Now I'm not pointing fingers at anyone but that murder/suicide story or report came from the same Sheriff's Department that test-fired Jerry's shotgun on Sunday behind the courthouse on November 10, 1974. The sheriff was still Jimmy Glass.

When Jerry Banks died, the newspapers made mention of a divorce being the central issue between Virginia and Jerry Banks.

During a series of phone calls, back and forth over the years, I quizzed Perry Banks about the day his brother died. I mentioned the divorce when he said, "Hold on, I'll call you right back."

Perry called me back, "I just got off the phone with Ludie. He said he had never heard anything about a divorce."

Neither Perry nor Ludie Banks had ever heard of a divorce or even a mentioning of a divorce by Virginia Banks.

Perry Banks' statement, 2009: "Jerry was living at home with Virginia and everything was fine considering what they had been through. Jerry asked once if I knew anything about Virginia and my brother-in-law Charles Crumbley. I told him I didn't know …

"Charles Crumbley left town and moved to Florida when Jerry came home.

"I do know for sure, Jerry was worried about something. After he came home, he carried a big gun in the car that Wade bought him. Jerry did not shoot himself. They did it.

"Jerry had no reason to kill himself. He knew there was going to be a large settlement."

I asked, "Do you think Jerry was afraid for his life or anything like that?"

Perry said, "I just don't know. He never talked about it."

⊕ ⊕ ⊕

This was not the first time someone from Henry County took a family member from the Banks family. Perry Banks remembered in 1961 the County Commissioner drove his car down the street where the Banks lived. He ran up into their front yard and ran over Jerry's three-year-old baby sister, Bevelin and killed her.

"He was so damn drunk the cops had to come drag him out of his car," Perry remarked.

Perry said, "I was only five years old at the time."

According to Ludie Banks, there was never a word spoken about this publicly. "They did come out and haul that drunk away in a sheriff's car and then they carried our baby sister away. It was horrifying for all us children to see our little baby sister's brains at the foot of our door steps."

CHAPTER 19

$12 Million Civil Action

UNITED STATES DISTRICT COURT, NORTHERN DISTRICT OF GEORGIA, ATLANTA DIVISION

The opinion of the court was delivered by: MOYE

Mr. Wade Crumbley represented Henry County, Georgia, in the capacity of assistant county attorney and county attorney from the summer of 1979 through January 1981. During this time Mr. Crumbley was representing Jerry Banks in the trial, State v. Banks (basically Henry County (Jimmy Glass) v. Jerry Banks). He was also representing Henry County at this time which means he was representing Sheriff Jimmy in the case Duffy v. Goins, No. C78-2208A (N.D.Ga.) Mr. Crumbley worked for Sheriff Glass, a defendant. The first matter that arose concerning the sheriff for County Attorney Crumbley was the case of Duffy v. Goins a civil rights action against Sheriff Glass, the City of McDonough, Georgia, certain of its officers, and Deputy Sheriff Ernest Wise. Henry County was not a named defendant. The complaint in Duffy with respect to defendant Glass alleged that Sheriff Glass, acting under color of state law, subjected plaintiff to cruel and unusual punishment and deprived plaintiff of his liberty and the security of his person without due process of law, in violation of and contrary to the Fourth, Eighth, and Fourteenth Amendments to the United States Constitution. The alleged actions were allegedly motivated by racial prejudice and an intent to deprive plaintiff of equal protection of the law. Duffy v. Goins, No. C78-2208A (N.D.Ga.), Complaint at P 33, filed December 27, 1978. Defendant Glass was further alleged to be liable to plaintiff (1) for his failure to adequately train, supervise, discipline, and control defendants Wise and Doe, who were deputy sheriffs of Henry County, id. at P 38, and (2) for malicious arrest and false imprisonment in violation of Ga. Code Ann. ?? 26-1308 and 1309.

My hat is off to Attorney Wade Crumbley for being able to carry out such duties as representing Jimmy Glass one day and taking him to court the next. It takes a remarkable man to carry opposing responsibilities for opposing clients while properly representing both.

Attorney Wade Crumbley was also about to start wearing another hat. He and other lawyers were representing Jerry Banks' mother in the law suit. Mr. Wade Crumbley was not allowed to represent Jerry's mother in her civil suit.

He is truly an honorable servant to mankind.

$12 Million Civil Action

DODSON v. FLOYD

UNITED STATES DISTRICT COURT, NORTHERN DISTRICT OF GEORGIA, ATLANTA DIVISION

December 18, 1981

Nannie L. (Banks) DODSON, Administratrix of the Estate of Jerry Banks, Deceased,
v.
Tommy FLOYD, et al.

This is a civil action for compensatory and punitive damages brought by Nannie L. Dodson, Administratrix of the Estate of Jerry Banks, deceased, against Henry County, Georgia, Jimmy H. Glass, Sheriff of Henry County, Georgia, and five additional law enforcement officials of said county. The detailed complaint, brought pursuant to 42 U.S.C. ?? 1981, 1983, 1985(2) and (3), 1986 and 1988, bases jurisdiction on 28 U.S.C. ?? 1331 and 1343(1)-(4). It is alleged within the complaint that the acts and omissions of defendants caused Jerry Banks to be convicted of two counts of murder, sentenced to death, and incarcerated for over six years for a crime which he did not commit. Specifically, the complaint alleges the defendants:

(1) Deprived Plaintiff's decedent of his Fourteenth Amendment due process right to have disclosed to him exculpatory evidence known to the State;
(2) Deprived him of his rights under the Sixth and Fourteenth Amendments to have compulsory process of obtaining witnesses in his favor, to be confronted with witnesses against him and to effective assistance of counsel;
(3) Deprived him of his Fourteenth Amendment due process right not to have false and perjured testimony used against him;

(4) Deprived him of his Fourteenth Amendment due process right to have access to exculpatory physical evidence; and

(5) Deprived him of his Fourteenth Amendment right to equal protection of the law, and not to be prosecuted because of his race.

All of the above conduct was allegedly intentional, reckless, wanton, willful, and grossly negligent, and was maliciously, wantonly, and oppressively done.

The complaint alleges that from and after June 10, 1979, Banks discovered a large body of theretofore undisclosed, exculpatory evidence. All of this evidence was allegedly known to the defendants Floyd, Robbins, Howard, Barnes, and Glass, and had never been disclosed to Banks or his counsel, or to the District Attorney and his assistants. None of the exculpatory evidence described was ever voluntarily disclosed by the defendants, according to the complaint, but was discovered from third parties and by judicial process. None of the exculpatory evidence was presented at Banks' two trials.

Mr. (Bobby Lee) Cook was not involved in this case as counsel for plaintiff until approximately a week to ten days prior to the filing of the complaint. On that day Mr. Crumbley and Mr. Harrison traveled to Mr. Cook's office in Summerville, Georgia, and spent about three hours summarizing the facts of the case for Mr. Cook. …. A few days later … Crumbley and Harrison drew the complaint for plaintiff, they returned to Summerville at which time Mr. Cook read and signed the complaint. …

This lawsuit was filed by the famed Attorneys Bobby Lee Cook and Stephen Harrison on behalf of the three children. Bobby Lee Cook is the first lawyer who defended Jim Williams, in his first trial down in Savannah. Jim Williams was portrayed by Kevin Spacey in <u>Midnight in the Garden of Good and Evil</u>.

He also defended several gentlemen from Knoxville, Tennessee, during the World's Fair fiasco years ago. Bobby Lee Cook is the real-life 'Matlock.' Other than that, he is just another run-of-the-mill lawyer who doesn't cotton to losing. This lawsuit started out in the millions of dollars but for some unknown reason the children were only awarded $150,000 for their unnecessary loss of both mother and father. Jimmy Glass and five of his men were sued for their deeds and the county insurance paid Mrs. Banks. And the defendants kept their jobs!

⊕ ⊕ ⊕

One detail here that I've seen printed in several documents is the statement "against Henry County, Georgia, Jimmy H. Glass, Sheriff of Henry County, Georgia, and five additional law enforcement officials of said county."

I have only read of Sheriff Jimmy Glass, four of his officers and the fourth member being Tommy Floyd. The defendants were said to be Floyd, Robbins, Howard, Barnes, and Glass; the fifth was not mentioned.

Why Floyd received top billing in this law suit is beyond my understanding. In fact, the fact that he was named in this action period was a total surprise to me.

⊕ ⊕ ⊕

CHAPTER 20

Jimmy, Jimmy

Before you judge people who were involved with events in this book, I believe there were some people who went along with the program, rather than against it. Case in point; remember Billy Payne and what happened to him.

Sheriff Jimmy Glass ran for public office as the Henry County Sheriff in 1972 and won hands down. He was born and raised in this area and before running for office had been selling insurance. Sheriff Cook was in office for a number of years. I have been told Jimmy Glass really brought in the votes. It has been said if Jimmy Glass ran for office today, he would get elected. There are some people in this region today who would vote for him in a heartbeat. By the same token they would be the ones to ridicule this book.

It was March of 1981 when Jerry Banks was killed. It was only three months later in June when Jimmy Glass's machine started misfiring.

According to his explanation, he was innocent. "I was not a party to any drug deal. I was working this case from the inside. I was undercover and the FBI entered the case without my knowledge. I was set up. I was framed." Well those were not Jimmy Glass's exact words but that is the way I heard it. That's right, framed. Yet he was caught red-handed and he cried foul.

According to Federal Court documents:

In the spring of 1981, Probate Judge Larry Tew, also a practicing attorney in Henry County was hired by Ed Black and John Harthorn to represent them against charges of smuggling drugs into the county. He got so involved with these two individuals that they all began hatching a scheme to fly more drugs into our local airstrip themselves. He must have been one of the good old boys and therefore knew how things worked and which palms needed greasing.

Well, to start, he went directly to Jimmy Glass and had "a set down." This discussion was about having access to Berry Hill Airstrip, out on Miller's Mill Road and to land planes loaded with drugs with police protection. First things, first; Jimmy Glass threw out a figure of "fifty thousand for me. I think some people get that much money for allowing for something like that."

I guess they had some kind of blue book for pricing that kind of activity.

That was the figure Mr. Tew took back to the two new clients he was representing in their previous drug deal.

I wonder how that works when you're already being charged with drug smuggling and you are about to shoot your other foot completely off.

Anyway, the two clients agreed to pay the price, sofa change compared to the amount of money this job would yield. Jimmy Glass went into action by calling his people in on the deal. Bill Hinton was not a problem. He was onboard. He owned the local airstrip. Bill Hinton was my VA inspector when I built homes in the price range where VA loans were needed. Let's just say I knew Bill Hinton.

Back to Glass: Who did he go to next but McDonough's Chief of Police, Hershel Childs, who would be the buffer between Jimmy Glass and all the action. In September 1981, a plane load of drugs landed at Berry Hill Airport. This was an easy fifty grand for Glass. This action would make Jimmy Glass guilty of importing methaqualone, a recreational drug commonly known as quaaludes.

For some unknown reason, their pilot decided he was out of the drug trade and these boys needed another pilot. Ed Black offered the job to a pilot named Ron Hoover, who put them off because he had to think about it overnight. Ron Hoover contacted the DEA and they contacted the FBI. Ron Hoover introduced Ed Black and Judge Larry Tew to a pilot who would take the job, an undercover agent for the Federal Bureau of Investigation. Larry Tew set up everything. He worked out the details with his new partner on flying the drugs into Berry Hill Airport and he also informed the pilot that arrangements had been taken care of with Jimmy Glass and Police Chief Childs. Childs would personally secure the airstrip and would provide the pilot with information regarding state and federal agents in the area. The pilot had a helper; he would work on the ground to unload the drugs. This was another backup undercover FBI agent.

Tew also informed the (undercover FBI) pilot that Sheriff Jimmy Glass knew everything going on and insured him everything would go smoothly. This was excellent news to the pilot.

On November 3, 1981, the next shipment of drugs landed at Berry Hill Airstrip in Henry County, Georgia, under the protection of Police Chief Childs and the County Sheriff Jimmy Glass. When the plane landed, it was unloaded and suitcases full of flour were unloaded by the backup agent in the presence of Childs. The two of them took the suitcases to a motel room to meet with Larry Tew and the undercover pilot. They were all arrested and after Childs and Tew knew there was no way out, they agreed to work with the FBI in hopes of a sweeter deal.

Phone calls were made to Bill Hinton by Larry Tew to make arrangements to deliver Hinton's share of the protection money. Sheriff Jimmy Glass was called by the Chief of Police Childs and the following conversation was recorded by the FBI:

Childs: Mr. Sheriff.
Glass: Yeah.
Childs: How are you?
Glass: Fine.
Childs: Good. Okay. A plane came in that I unloaded and went to Atlanta with it.
Glass: Okay.

Childs: I reckon we get our money tomorrow.
Glass: Okay.
Childs: Did everything go all right down there?
Glass: Yeah.
Childs: No problems?
Glass: Huh-uh (negative).
Childs: Alright. I will talk to you in the morning then.
Glass: Okay.

The only thing Jimmy got the next morning was the FBI at his door. Jimmy Glass was arrested and another charge was added for conspiring to import methaqualone and cocaine. If it had not been for Ron Hoover's actions, there is no telling how many more loads Jimmy Glass would have dumped onto our streets. The oil had just run out of Jimmy's machine.

On November 4th Sheriff Jimmy Glass was arrested by the FBI out of Atlanta. Though this arrest had nothing to do with Jerry Banks, Mr. Glass's true face was exposed to the world.

Jimmy Glass accused Judge Tew and Police Chief Childs of conspiring against him and denied talking to Mr. Childs the night before. Jimmy Glass also contended the FBI undercover agents lied under oath. He introduced numerous character witnesses; two were surely there for the sole purpose of bolstering his character. The Georgia House Speaker Thomas Murphy and the ex-United States Senator Herman Talmadge took the stand and testified on behalf of Jimmy Glass as to his good character. By Jimmy Glass bringing in these witnesses as to his character, it allowed the Government not only to question them about his character but it also allowed them to bring in their own witnesses as well.

The Government wasted no time during cross-examination of these witnesses by questioning them specifically if they were aware of Jimmy Glass' involvement in his supposed "ticket-fixing" for money practice related to traffic violations. But then in rebuttal they put Jimmy Glass's former secretary on the stand. She told the court how Jimmy Glass would have mothers come into the office and leave plain white envelopes with money inside in order to drop their child's drug charges.

Jimmy, Jimmy

✜ ✜ ✜

After convicted felon and known drug-trafficker Jimmy Glass went to Federal Prison, the Governor of the State of Georgia appointed Atlanta Police Officer Donald Chaffin as Sheriff of Henry County. Donald Chaffin, a life-long resident of Henry County, served honorably for twenty seven years. As I understand it, he too grew up in Kelleytown.

I recently asked Retired Sheriff Donald Chaffin, who knew of the Jerry Banks case, why didn't anyone reopen the King and Hartsfield case. Was there a particular reason? He responded, "I don't know. You know, I just don't know. You would have to ask the District Attorney."

Bill Hinton died shortly after entering prison and Jimmy Glass served his time and was released. My understanding was he served all or part of ten years. It was rumored that he was free for a while but one day the FBI pulled up to the barber shop in McDonough where Glass was working giving prison-style haircuts and revoked his parole on the spot for associating with known felons. He returned to prison and later was released again.

There is an old saying, history repeats itself. I don't know, but Jimmy Glass had a chance of repeating history to some degree. His great-grandfather Newton A. Glass was the Sheriff of Henry County in the 1890s and well into the early 1900s. From all things written about him, I would have to say that he was one of the most distinguished sheriffs in the history of this County.

✜ ✜ ✜

Around 2007 or 2008, I was well into this book and my plans were to wait near the end and call Jimmy Glass. I could not seem to contain myself so one day I placed a call. His wife answered and said he was out. Boy, I was glad. A few days later I called back and she put him on the line. He was as normal as any other 76-year-old man but sounded much younger.

I explained I was writing a book about Henry County and I knew his great-grandfather was once the Sheriff around the end of the 1800s. I went on to explain how I had read he was known as a great man and a legend as a Sheriff in Henry County. He seemed proud of that fact and his response was an affirmation to these facts.

I questioned him about little things, small talk. He told me he was born and raised in nearby Flippen, Georgia and he had lived in Henry County all his life. He told me he had been in insurance before becoming Sheriff.

I ran out of little things to bother Jimmy Glass with, so I did it.

"You remember Jerry Banks' case, don't you?"

"Oh yes, very well," he said.

"Did you ever think that someone else might have murdered King and Hartsfield?"

You can see I'm playing softball here.

"Ah, you know I never really thought Jerry Banks would be found guilty for those murders."

"Well, did you ever think that King was involved in something that got him killed, like drugs or something like that?"

"Yes, I admit that was always in the back of my mind. I did think about that, but you know, I kept real close to that investigation, everything that went on, and there was never anything that came up that led us in that direction."

Now it was time to play hardball.

"Well, you remember Detective Phillip Howard?"

"Oh yes, I remember him. Phillip worked for me."

"Well, you say you felt Banks was innocent. How was it that Howard was able to convict him?"

This changed his tone a bit and he started dancing around with his answer, so I went for broke.

"You know there are statements and evidence out there to show that Phillip Howard falsified the shell evidence in ..."

"Wait just a damn minute here. Just who in the Hell am I talking to?"

At this time he was having a hydraulic fit.

"What is your name? Where in the hell do you live? I want to know where you live. You're coming out of the dark asking some mighty dark questions? Why don't you come over here and ask me to my face? I want to know where you live. I want to know ... who you are? Where do you live ...?"

With every outburst, his voice got louder and louder. I could feel the anger from which I had never known as he went on and on for awhile like a bottle rocket out of control.

"I'm sorry but it sounds like I may have struck a nerve with you ... Mr. Glass ... A minute ago you said you thought Jerry was innocent and now I'm just trying to show you that I know damn-good-and-well he was innocent and now you're threatening me." Like I said, he seemed out of control ... then he finally hung up the phone.

"Where do you live?" *That was scary as hell. I wonder what would have happened if I had told him?*

PART VI:
A MAN SEPARATED FROM HIS SOUL

CHAPTER 21

A Misty Morning

Around five years after the second trial, Jerry Banks was brought back from Jackson State Prison to McDonough. His new lawyers had filed for an extraordinary motion to get a third trial. Jerry took the stand during this hearing. I read much of Jerry's words on the stand that day and they were words that rang with truth and honesty, unlike those who railroaded him. They could "not remember", they could "not recall", they were "not aware." They were seasoned professionals and all of a sudden they didn't know their own butts from fat meat.

I genuinely don't think it was Alzheimer's and it didn't have anything to do with record-keeping.

While on the stand on December 22, 1980, Jerry stated they took his shotgun from him at his house on the morning of the 8th of November, 1974, at 5:00 a.m.

> Q. Do you remember who took your shotgun?
> A. No! All I remember ... the officer was skinny.
> *Pay close attention. This is where it gets good. Re-read Jerry's last statement and remember it.*
> Q. He was asked. "Can you tie that date to anything in particular?

A. Yes, sir, I remember that day because it was misting rain and it was early in the morning after the murders.

They first took him downtown for his witness statement at midnight. They took him back home in the early morning hours. This would be right about 5:00 a.m. the morning after the murders, as stated by the Sheriff's Department in court. This would be hours before the evidence shells were found in full daylight on the 8th of November. Now it's been six years and Jerry is testifying about a moment in time that may have taken less than fifteen minutes. When I read *misting* rain, something happened.

I didn't know at the time why Jerry's statement about the misting rain stood out so much but it did. I thought about his statement throughout the day and that night. Jerry was in my head again. It finally hit me between my eyes.

I knew this statement was particularly valuable, it was typical Jerry Banks. To me it was as though Jerry were speaking from the grave, "Prove I'm telling the truth about the rain and you will prove they were lying about picking up my gun on Sunday." This became a challenge which became more powerful than the book itself.

Jerry had been accused of killing two people in an exceptionally brutal manner usually reserved for hit men. Jerry Banks had been accused of stealing Marvin King's money from his wallet and then lying about it. He had been accused of hunting with a non-regulation dog, according to Ed McGarity. These three things were the reason Jerry Banks would have had thousands of volts connected to a wet skull cap on his head. Not one of which were true. Jerry Banks did lie when he said he loaned his gun to another man, but he was no killer. Jerry's latest lawyers had already shown the only real evidence against him (the three shells) had been planted and the withholding of all those witness statements amounted to a lot more than lies.

It's the smallest things that make the biggest differences. Near the end of my research, Jerry had me looking through hell and high water for someone who could give me a weather report for Stockbridge, Georgia, on the day of November 8, 1974, at 5:00 a.m.

I imagined I would call the Weather Station. "Hello, this is Mr. Sargent. Could you please check your records and ... No, no, no, not just any weather report, much further back, say 1974, and one that would show just the slightest bit of untraceable precipitation in the air at 5:00 am. And let me give you the man's address."

I wish it had been that easy!

I thought this would be something next to impossible but the uncanny thing about it was the way I approached this task, as though I were going outside to get the mail.

For some indescribable reason, I felt this report was out there waiting for me.

I have provided for you a three-page document I finally tracked down in June of 2010 from NOAA's National Climate Center in Asheville, North Carolina. After I found it, with the assistance of Meteorologist William Brown, I found another needle in another haystack.

The documents below are the weather data reports for the Henry County area in the year 1974 and specifically for the month of November. Keep in mind, Jerry said it was 5:00 a.m. and it was misting. If you examine the top portion of the document, **Figure 21.1**, you will see in the middle of the data a column "**precipitation**". On the far left you will see **"Date"**. Now move down to the 8th and under precipitation, column 10 **"water equivalent/ inches"**. You will see the letter **"T"**. Meteorologist William Brown informed me "T" indicates an amount too small to measure.

In Georgia we call that a mist.

Sins of Henry County

LOCAL CLIMATOLOGICAL DATA
U.S. DEPARTMENT OF COMMERCE
NATIONAL OCEANIC AND ATMOSPHERIC ADMINISTRATION
ENVIRONMENTAL DATA SERVICE
LATITUDE 33° 38' N   LONGITUDE 84° 26' W   ELEVATION (GROUND) 10

Figure 21.1
Precipitation Water Equivalent Inches
Source: NOAA's National Climate Center in Asheville North Carolina

That means on the 8th of November there was a *trace* of rain. That however does not indicate at what time this occurred. I needed to find out the time of this "T".

If you look at the next section, **Figure 21.2**, you will see **"Observations at 3-hr Intervals"**. Under **"Weather"** at the

A Misty Morning

top-middle of that data, Go down to the date 08 and you will see an **"R"**. Rain, that's good, but it's not a mist, and if you follow that over to the far left you will see under **"Hour"** that it occurred at 07 or 0700 hr. (That's 7 am). William Brown also informed me that by the "T" at the top of the first page, on the 8th means again that it was too small to measure. Therefore he said that tells him that at 7:00 a.m. that morning of November the 8th there was a 2 or 3-minute rain. Now again, this is not a misting rain and the time doesn't fit either. It's too late in the morning.

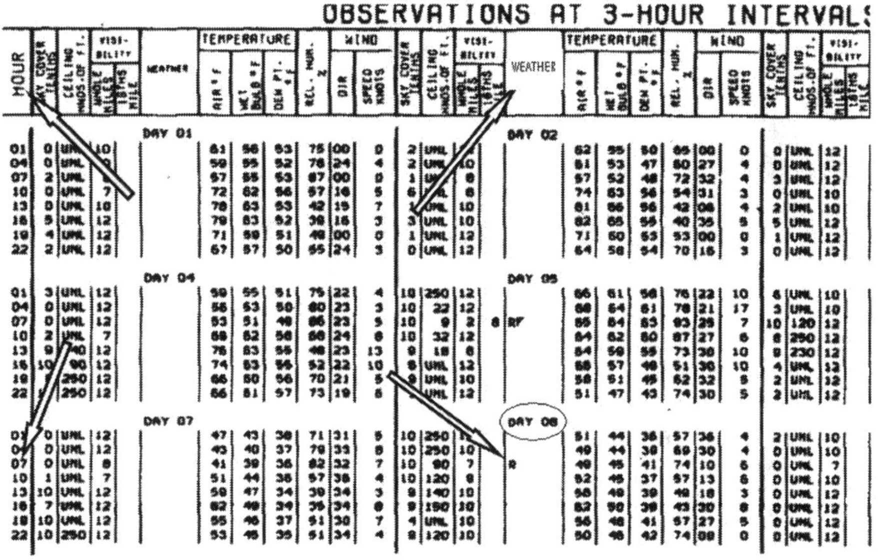

Figure 21.2
Observations at 3-Hour Intervals
Source: NOAA's National Climate Center in Asheville North Carolina

Now here is where the hair on the back of my neck started doing its thing. Please follow me to **Figure 21.3**, titled **"Hourly Precipitation"**. Again the dates are on the left. On the 8th day of November 1974, it started "T"ing at 5:00 a.m. until 8:00 a.m. You can also see that, other than that day, it did not mist again until the 14th of November. There was no mist or rain on Sunday November the 10th. Jerry Banks was not lying about the police picking the gun up at 5 a.m., the morning of November 8, 1974.

HOURLY PRECIPITATION (WATER EQUIVALENT IN INCHES)

Date	A. M. HOUR ENDING AT											
	1	2	3	4	5	6	7	8	9	10	11	12
1												
2												
3												
4												
5			T		T	T	.14	.16	.01	.01	T	
6												
7												
8					T	T	T	T				
9												
10												
11												
12												
13												
14									T	T	T	.01
15												
16												
17					T	T	T	T				
18	.05	.03	.04	.01	.09	T	T	T	T	T		
19												
20		T	T	T	T	T	.22	.12	T	.08	T	
21												
22												
23												
24												
25						T	T		T	T		
26												
27												
28												
29												
30								T	T	.04	.15	.20

P. M. HOUR ENDING AT												Date
1	2	3	4	5	6	7	8	9	10	11	12	
												1
												2
												3
												4
												5
												6
												7
												8
												9
												10
T	T	.04	.04	.37	.19	.16	.03	T				11
												12
												13
	T	.06	.05	.06	.06	.04	.03	T				14
												15
										T		16
								T	.29	.14	.15	17
												18
						T	.01					19
												20
												21
												22
												23
												24
												25
												26
												27
												28
												29
.29	.19	.29	.03	T	T	T	T	T	T	.01	T	30

Figure 21.3
Hourly Precipitation (Water Equivalent in Inches)
Source: NOAA's National Climate Center in Asheville North Carolina

Jerry's words about that morning go hand in hand with Bud Kelley's statement. There was no test-fire session behind the courthouse on Sunday November 10, 1974, and there was no church service to disturb. Could this mean they were lying under oath, all of them?

I think this was particularly relevant to Jerry because they were taking his father's old gun out in that weather. It was old and only a single shot. It did not work like a new gun and it had a lot of old electrical tape holding it together, but it had been handed down from Mr. Banks, who may not have been his father, but he died serving his country and he was a good man. Jerry was a good man also.

CHAPTER 22

What Did He Know and When Did He know It

Personally, I see everything in this case differently. A fair trial ... not a fair trial, motive ... no motive and evidence withheld ... not withheld, that is not all that I see in those statements. It is not a question of did they do anything or how they did this, that or whatever. The only question I have is, "Why."

Why was Jerry Banks framed? Why would Lead Detective Phillip Howard and others want to frame him? It appears to me that others may have lied under oath to allow it to happen, not once but in two trials.

As the old saying goes, what did Lead Detective Howard know and when did he know it?

During the first and subsequent trial, Exhibit #14, the red sweater worn by Melanie was being discussed by Kelly Fite.

BY MR.CRAIG: (DURING THE SECOND TRIAL)

> Q. All right, would you remove that (the red sweater) from the bag itself and hold it up. What did you do with the particular red sweater that came out of State's Exhibit #14?

A. Well there is a gunshot hole of entry in the back of the sweater and this is what I paid special attention to.
Q. All right, what was the purpose of your examining that red sweater?
A. Well, it was to get an idea or to determine the muzzle-to-target distance or the distance from the end of the shotgun to the clothing and also, examination of this hole also indicated to me the type of ammunition used to make this hole.
Q. And how did it do that?
A. Well, in Winchester Western type buckshot, they pack the buckshot in polyethylene granules and this keeps the shot from banging against each other and deforming with the purpose of making the shot firing more accurate. I notice there are numerous particles, of this polyethylene, granules on the ... around the entry hole in the back of the sweater.
Q. The polyethylene particles that you found in the sweater; are they peculiar to Winchester Western shells. Are they unique or does any other manufacturer use that same type packing?
A. Well, they are unique to Winchester Western type buckshot.

BY THE COURT: (JUDGE SOSEBEE)

Q. Mr. Fite, did you have an occasion to form an opinion as to the distance of the muzzle of the gun from the sweater that you examined?
A. Yes, sir, I did, I fired test patterns with State's Exhibit #1, the 12-gauge shotgun, and compared these tests with Winchester Western 00 buckshot and compared my test with holes shown in this sweater and I came to the conclusion that the muzzle-to-target distance was approximately five feet.

What Kelly Kite, from the Georgia Bureau of Investigation, explained to the court was that he and only he had to examine

What Did He Know and When Did He know It

the hole in the back of Melanie's sweater in order to discover numerous particles of the polyethylene granules that are unique to Winchester Western, 00 buck shotgun shells. Meaning there was no other shotgun shell that could have been used in at least Melanie's murder.

I know what Detective Phillip Howard did with Jerry's gun, and I know when he did it. With no hesitation on my part, I'm going to cast caution to the wind and ask the most fundamental question of all. Where and when did he obtain the knowledge needed to pull it off? Using Jerry's own shotgun during the early morning hours of that Friday to falsify and plant evidence is one thing. Knowing the exact type shell to use in order to match victims wounds is the most fundamental question.

If Phillip Howard played the shell game with the first two rounds (said to be found at the scene on the 8th) and then later with the third shell (said to be found on the 13th), how did he know to fire Winchester Western 00 through Jerry's gun, instead of some other 12-gauge brand like Remington 00, Federal 00, Peterson 00, Hornady, Fiocci or any number of other manufacturers from around the world which were available in this country? There are endless numbers of 12-gauge rounds he could have picked. A number of at least 40 different manufacturers were given to me by a gun-shop owner. Any other manufacturer or type would *not* have matched with the unique evidence and therefore Jerry Banks would have never been arrested.

If Howard had *not* planted the exact shells, then Kelly Fite would have called from the GBI Office informing Tommy Floyd, "We have good news and bad news".

"The good news, the shells found at the murder scene indeed came from Jerry's gun.

But the bad news, they were not used to kill the two victims."

This is why the same unique type of ammunition used in the murders had to be fired through Jerry's gun in order to seal the deal.

Okay! The shell evidence was planted. Let's move on.

Review the time line. The question is now, how did he know to use the same unique type of ammunition? Answer that and think about it.

Do you believe the odds of picking the same ammunition was a lucky guess?

What would that tell you if it was not a lucky guess?

What if it was shown that it would be highly unlikely Phillip Howard guessed about the Winchester Western brand?

Could it be that he knew ... because he already knew?

You see, Phillip Howard's planting of the shells would not be as valuable to me as "how did he know" to use the manufacturer, brand, and type which would match up with the State's findings. In conversation with Attorney Buddy Welch about this matter, it was and is his position that Phillip Howard got the information from the Crime Laboratory and asked what type shells were used in the killings. Buddy Welch believed Howard asked the night of the murders during or after the autopsies which did not begin until 11 p.m. and carried on well into the early morning hours. I don't think so. Evidence examinations were Kelly Fite's responsibility and he was *not* present the night of the autopsies. It wasn't until Friday, November 8, that Kelly Fite examined Melanie's red sweater under a microscope. Phillip Howard could have found out the size of the pellets, 00 buck, but that's all. It wasn't until the next day, after the evidence shells were found at the murder site by Detective Phillip Howard and Detective Ted Ray that Kelly Fite knew anything himself.

Remember the statement that Myers worked so hard to get Dr. Howard to say on the stand without leading him?

> Q. In other words, the question I'm asking, in determining cause, you do not also identify weapon?
> Q. All right, you identify gauge?
> Q. Now, which did you do?
> Q. That's what I wanted to know, I wanted to know if you had made a determination.
> Q. You did not make a determination?

A. ...but I didn't make this determination myself; other people in the Crime Lab did; are you with me?

Dr. Howard testified "but I didn't make this determination myself; other people in the Crime Lab did (make this determination); are you with me (do you understand, I needed Kelly Fite to determine that it was Winchester Western 00 buck.)" There is no way Detective Howard could have gotten this information from Dr. Howard the night of the autopsies.

In another statement Dr. Howard from the GBI stated that he had removed pellets and wadding from Marvin King's midsection and took them to Kelly Fite the next day. This was State Exhibit # 26. That exhibit along with Melanie's red sweater allowed Kelly Fite to determine which type of shell was used by the killer. It was Winchester Western 12-gauge 00 buck.

I find it hard to believe that this work could have been completed by 9 a.m. on the morning of November 8, 1974.

How could Phillip Howard guess the exact type shells to send to Atlanta? It's almost like he already knew, himself, the type of shells used to kill Marvin King and Melanie Hartsfield on November 7, 1974. If you explore the time line, there was not a lot of time to go out and purchase shotgun shells between the time of the autopsies (well into the morning hours) and the time Commissioner Bud Kelley heard the three blasts (courthouse opened at 8:00 a.m.) the next morning.

What place of business would be open at 7:00 a.m. to allow someone to purchase ammunition and return to the courthouse by 8:00 a.m.?

I have said it before and I'll say it again, they were not in the closing-the-case mode, they were in the cover-up mode.

I have read so many times almost 300 pages of just the 2nd trial. I think I could quote statements in my sleep. These 3 shells were the most talked-about items in both trials, in all the hearings and appeals, and all the appearances before the Georgia and U.S. Supreme Court. In all cases where a description was rendered by lawyers, judges, police and even the GBI experts, not one person used any other description of those shells other than Winchester Western 00 12-gauge. Some added the term "Buck Shot."

Remember how proudly Phillip Howard rattled off his description of the three evidence shells offered in front of him in court?

A. They are Winchester Western XX Super X 00 Buck, Mark V shotgun casing, 12-gauge,

Again, what did Lead Detective Howard know and when did he know it?

CHAPTER 23

A Conspiracy in Henry County

Let me tell you more of what I believe happened on November 7, 1974.

I truly believe on that November day, in Henry County, Georgia, there was a conspiracy to have Marvin King and Melanie Ann Hartsfield executed. And it came from people within Henry County.

The principals knew that Thursday morning Melanie Ann Hartsfield attended her morning class at Clayton Jr. College in the city of Morrow and Marvin King had his first period Band Class at Jonesboro High School. Both of their classes got out around 10:30 a.m. There were witnesses at the College saying Miss Hartsfield told them she was going to meet Mr. King that morning around 10:30 a.m. and then she was supposed to be at Riverdale Elementary at noon, where she worked as a part-time choir director. In talking to long-time Jonesboro High School Principal Fred Smith, he said Mr. King left after his first class at 10:30 a.m. When Miss Hartsfield did not make her appointment at noon, the school called her parents, who in turn called the Clayton County police. At that time a missing person's report was filed and this went out over the radio in both counties.

Sins of Henry County

⊕ ⊕ ⊕

For some reason, either by request from someone she and King knew or more than likely by force, Melanie Ann drove her car to Stockbridge 10 to 15 miles away. **See Figure 8: Routes Taken by Miss Hartsfield and Mr. King.** She only had an hour and a half before she needed to be at work. She would have known if she drove to Stockbridge and back to Riverdale, round trip without stopping, she would be late for work. Thus I don't think she went willingly. I would not rule out at gun-point.

After arriving in Stockbridge, she was detained elsewhere for a brief conversation away from her car. When she returned to her car, it would not start.

Her father, Charles Hartsfield, said he thought it was the battery but when he raised the hood, the coil wire had been pulled. "I plugged it in and it started right up."

I believe this was a well-planned murder conspiracy. Melanie Hartsfield was used for the purpose of drawing Marvin King across the county line into Henry County. I cannot say they all knew each other as a group but they knew she would call Marvin King and she did.

Marvin King drove to Stockbridge to aid Melanie Hartsfield. There were people who wanted Marvin King for some reason. He knew who they were and what they wanted. Marvin King and possibly Melanie Hartsfield knew something that got them killed. Somebody did not want them to be killed in Clayton County. In order to have control over this situation, the Clayton County police could not be involved.

I believe Mr. King had uncovered the underground life style and the activities of people in power through his relationship with long-time friend Detective Mark Foster from Griffin, Georgia. I believe Marvin King had to be silenced.

Marvin King left the Jonesboro area around 11:15 a.m. driving toward Stockbridge. **See Figure 8: Routes Taken by Miss Hartsfield and Mr. King.** The closest route would have been Highway 138 East. Arriving somewhere around 11:45 a.m., he found Miss Hartsfield at Mays Corner (a shopping strip) in

Stockbridge. Under normal circumstances he at least would have raised the hood while she cranked the engine.

They left the area in his car as fast as he got there but Marvin King took an odd route back to Clayton County. Instead of taking the shorter route Highway 138 West, he dropped down south on Highway 42 several miles and turned west on Hudson Bridge Road (now known as Eagles' Landing). This route was much longer. It was not known if King was trying to sneak back across the county line or if he was forced to take another route. Maybe he knew they would be looking for them on Highway 138. They never made it back across Interstate I-75 or the Clayton County line.

Around 12:00 noon a station wagon was seen by a witness, Frank Walker, who recalled having seen two cars, one cream-colored Chevy he took to be an unmarked detective's car by its antennas, and the other a dark-colored, small station wagon on a road about a half mile from the scene of the murders. **See Figure 5: Aerial Photograph of Crime scene.** A woman, sitting in the passenger side of the station wagon, was trying to pull the smaller of the two men back into that car. The two men were facing each other and clearly arguing.

At gun-point Marvin King and Melanie Ann Hartsfield either drove or were driven a short distance away. It was only a right turn onto Rock Quarry Road then less than a mile down and a left turn onto the old roadbed.

It took another 2 hours to summon a white hit-man in a black van, wearing an army field coat with a Browning automatic shotgun.

Did I refer to him as the hit man? Bam......Bam................. Bam......Bam.

"I remembered hearing about a witness saying ... Four gunshots in rapid succession ...with a slight pause in between. ... " Charles Tomlinson told me.

Four gunshots in rapid succession sounds a lot like five to six seconds total. A Browning automatic shotgun does not mean it is an automatic gun; it means it loads each shell automatically rather than having to be loaded manually, like Jerry's.

Seven people, two of whom were police officers, heard the shotgun blast at 2:30 p.m. One of those witnesses drove by and saw a white man standing alongside the road at the murder site smoking a cigarette with his foot propped up on the bumper of the black van with a Browning automatic shotgun under his arm.

Three hours later, after the murders, Jerry Banks and his cousin Mamian Webster Jr. were finishing up their day of hunting, when Jerry's little puppy discovered the bodies. They had different views on what to do that day. Jerry stayed and Mamian ran home. Around 5 a.m. the next morning after taking his statement and his boots, someone from the Henry County Sheriff's Office took Jerry back home in sock feet and unlawfully secured the old shotgun.

During that morning, sometime after the court house opened at 8 a.m., Lead Detective Phillip S. Howard fired Jerry's shotgun three times. Phillip Howard quickly made his way to the murder scene where others had been looking unsuccessfully for evidence since 4:00 a.m. Guess who found the first shell ... "... somewhere between 7:30 a.m. and 9:00 a.m. ..." Those were the words of Phillip S. Howard! And then, four to five minutes later another one. "I found one," yelled Detective Ted Ray.

The soonest Phillip Howard could have arrived at the crime scene after leaving the courthouse, if he left at 8:30 a.m., would be 8:45 to 9:00 that morning. The likelihood is he left the courthouse somewhere between 8:15 and 8:30 that morning in order for Bud Kelley to hear the three shots.

Phillip Howard held onto the third shell until December 13th when he arranged another search party over a month later. This time he invited two officers from Clayton County and two officers from the GBI. This would make a significant group to witness the finding of an additional shell at the crime scene that would be tied to Jerry's shotgun. This shell was to appear as though it had never been in the custody of the Henry County Sherriff's Office at any time. This shell was handed over at that spot to a GBI officer. It, too, of course, was a match to Jerry's shotgun.

But wait, they now had three shells from the crime scene but none of the so-called *test-fired* shells, or at least that is what the GBI thought. Phillip Howard had never sent the test-fired shells from November the 10th because there were none left; he had already used them. At some other time and place, Howard fired three more rounds from Jerry's shotgun and sent them to Atlanta for comparison. The day Phillip Howard finally got around to sending those shells to the Georgia Lab was December 2, 1974. Well over a month later. ...

I have always wondered, what happened to the fourth shell? It's very simple. All four of the original shells were policed by the hit-man. Hell, he may have been comfortable at what he was doing, where he was doing it and who was protecting him, but he was no fool. The only reason I believe any shells at all were found is because Phillip S. Howard placed them at the scene. He only fired three rounds at the courthouse, so that was all that were found at the scene.

Jerry Banks was not convicted on a mistaken identification by a confused witness. Jerry Banks was not convicted because of overwhelming, unfortunate but truthful circumstantial evidence. Jerry Banks was used as a decoy in order to hide the real reason Marvin King and Miss Melanie Ann Hartsfield were executed.

CHAPTER 24

D. A. Tommy Floyd

To say District Attorney Tommy Floyd played a small part in this story would be an understatement.

I believe I have walked on eggs around Detective Tommy Floyd's involvement in this murder case. I have stated time and time again that I personally did not believe that he was involved in anything wrong. Was I positive? Well, sort of. Was there just a little doubt anywhere, running around in my mind? I studied documents that are three decades old and I have no one to ask. I never had any real doubts or concerns, just unanswered questions.

From studying recorded facts, times, order of events in the time lines and each person's statements, I think Detective Tommy Floyd was possibly the only honest investigator working the case while others kept him in the dark as their plan unfolded.

If this were true, why did I wait until last to interview District Attorney Tommy Floyd? To tell you the truth, I finished the book and sent my editor a blank chapter. There was no text.

"Are you saying you're going to tell this story without interviewing District Attorney Tommy Floyd? Why," she asked.

I can't exactly put my finger on it, but, "Yes ... I'm done. It is over. I cannot keep asking questions about this murder case. At some point his story will have to come out after the book is published. I am afraid to do anymore interviews. I am not afraid of D.A. Floyd. I worry about others in town who may hear of our interview, people in high places, who very well may be in town today."

On November 28, 2011, I walked into the Henry County District Attorney's Office held by D.A. Tommy Floyd. Somehow, I had convinced myself this was the right thing to do. If I were going to publish this book and claim that I had thoroughly investigated every aspect of this case, I had to include D.A. Tommy Floyd. After all, my goodness, he was the arresting officer of Jerry Banks and he is our District Attorney today.

His assistant had been told twice the purpose of my visit ... I was writing a book about Jerry Banks. Therefore I was comfortable in knowing he knew my reason for being there, but as I approached his desk, he asked, "Who are you and what do you want?"

It was too late. I was there. I truly felt I was in the presence of someone who did not like me. First of all, he made me feel as though I had been caught in his kitchen, going through all of his drawers and utensils. By the look on his face, I could feel he was thinking, "Who is this yo-yo, wanting to come in here and ask me all these questions?"

That would be understandable. But, feelings aside, this was something that needed to be done. After hearing those words in that tone, I forgot all about how I was going to lead with a statement of how I, in no way, had any intentions of embarrassing him or asking any questions that might be inappropriate. After all, I realized the position he was in 35 years ago and his position today. Even though I felt unwelcomed, my plan hadn't completely gone out the window. However, as far as asking for his approval to record this conversation ... that did go out the window as I carefully and boldly did so.

As I found myself fumbling around with my recorder, he was already explaining "(It was all based on) Banks' shotgun being a 12-gauge (which he happened to have with him) when he reported to Eberhardt ... and I ... I went to his house and seized the gun ..."

I foolishly interrupted without realizing what he had just told me, "Do you know what ever happened to the gun?"

"No! No I didn't. He was brought to the station that night for a statement, the gun was fired ... the shells were sent to the Crime Lab <u>where they stayed until December</u>."

Now I would have jumped up and started yelling and dancing around his office because I was given first-hand testimony that proves Jerry Banks was not only innocent but he was framed. The only problem was, at that time, I had not heard a word he said. I could not get those words out of my head, "Who are you and what do you want?" But at least it was recorded.

The interview did not go well, but the information was earth-shattering. Soon I rebounded and learned he still believed Jerry Banks killed Marvin King and Miss Hartsfield.

Does that mean I was behind enemy lines? No! It only means Tommy Floyd was lied to by Jimmy Glass, Dick Barnes, Paul Robbins and Phillip Howard and he never read the trial transcripts. For Sgt. Floyd to be kept in the dark by the Henry County Sheriff's Department was one thing, but for him to serve under the Henry County Prosecutor and still not be privy to the above-mentioned officers and their deeds means someone else wasn't completely honest with the cleanest cop of the force either.

"I don't think he acted alone though," he said.

"Well, Jerry wasn't alone that day when he found the bodies," I told D.A. Floyd

"Who was with him, his brother?" he asked.

This was not a surprise. Perry Banks had always told me that Sgt. Tommy Floyd suspected he was the killer.

"No, it was his cousin Mamian Webster Jr."

"Well, there was no record of that."

"Well it was all in the hidden file ..." when I was interrupted.

"What hidden file are you talking about?"

"You remember Bill Hart taking the file with him when he left Henry County ..."

"No I don't know anything about a hidden file."

Well, the interview pretty well went downhill from there. I am sure the length of time passing was a factor and he said it had been a long time. I did not want him to know the depth of my knowledge about this case. His memory served him well but his version of a few of the events fell a little short from what my investigation told me. For the most part they were minor details. However some were earth-shattering.

At one point he made a statement that sent cold chills down my back. We had been talking about the three shells being the heart of their case against Banks and how Detective Phillip Howard's credibility had been badly damaged.

We were not making good eye contact and I was flopping around like carp on a fishing dock with my questions. I could not think forward, for my next questions, because I couldn't get his answers out of the way in order to move on. He was doing okay. As I resurfaced, he was telling me of his time-line.

He said, "Kelly Fite called and told me to go get that gun because the shells did match ... I think that was when I executed the search warrant ...That was when we focused on Jerry Banks; he wasn't even in my picture until then."

I asked, "When everything unfolded (Jerry's release), did you ever feel like he was innocent, after he was released from prison?"

"No, I became more convinced ... that at least he was involved ... but the whole trial ... the more ... I mean, I had questions ... there was no real reason for it ... there was no apparent motive for him to kill anybody."

But he still felt Jerry Banks was guilty.

I asked, "Do you know why he was released from prison?"

"The case was naught."

He did not answer my question. I was expecting, "Yea, there was a boatload of witnesses who had been withheld ...."

But instead, he explained his reason. He went on to explain the second trial was reversed because of the lack of credibility of Detective Phillip Howard and the shell evidence.

Not true. And I'm not insinuating anything here, I'm just stating facts. The second trial was reversed because of all the witnesses who he never interviewed, because he was never made aware of them ....

"Myself and (Asst. D.A.) Harold Craig were charged with getting the case ready to try the third time."

D. A. Tommy Floyd

(*This was shortly after he left the Sheriff's Office and joined the D.A.'s Office.*)

Mr. Floyd was refreshing me with the same details that I had been writing poems about in my sleep. Basically how the Defense "claimed" they discovered Detective Phillip Howard's shell game.

He referred to Howard as Shug Howard, a nickname, and continued to tell how Shug's credibility had been severely damaged.

To paraphrase D.A. Floyd's repeated justification of Jerry Banks' release from prison, "Howard's credibility was so damaged that we could not go through a third trial, and we were not sure we believed him. And because we felt like we could not go forward with the trial ..."

I interrupted, "But doesn't it stand to reason that Howard was lying about test-firing on Sunday."

"Do you understand the meaning of the word credibility?" he snapped. "I said his credibility about the shell had been destroyed."

"Yes. I understand. But it wasn't destroyed enough for you to realize that Jerry quite possibly could have been innocent?"

Okay, he just gave me a lesson on the word "credibility." Now let's see if I have it right. Detective Phillip Howard has no credibility as to whether or not he falsified evidence in a death penalty case, yet when I ask if it would be possible if he was lying about the date and time he stated the test-firing took place ... D.A. Floyd got upset. Well, credibility should come into play when I ask "Wouldn't it stand to reason that there was a possibility that Jerry was innocent if Detective Howard were lying."

D.A. Tommy Floyd believed Shug's credibility was damaged, but not enough to change his thinking about the possibility of Jerry Banks being innocent. He still thinks Jerry Banks was guilty. That was the reason I kept asking about Howard's credibility. It had nothing to do with me not understanding the word's meaning.

He explained they could not verify the chain of custody as to the evidence shells or the shells fired behind the courthouse. "In my opinion ..., I think we talked to some of the officers at the scene ... they said I can tell you in my opinion that I saw him at this time ... I was familiar with the shells at this time, but we couldn't put it together as a testimonial standpoint ... we could not proceed."

Again, enough about not being able to prove Shug Howard was a bad cop.

I interrupted again. "Well, do you remember Bud Kelley?"

By the nod of his head, I took it as a yes. But it was not in the same sense as I was referring to Mr. Kelley. He knew Bud Kelley, and that was all.

"Well it was his testimony ... it was probably in a deposition ... in fact I think he did come forward to the D.A.'s Office at that time that he remembered Phillip Howard test-firing the three shells behind the courthouse ..."

"Oh, I witnessed it." he interrupted.

"You witnessed it?" I asked.

"I witnessed the test-firing, the shells that night ...or the next day, I'm not sure which.

"Holy Toledo! Stop the press!" I'm thinking.

"You ... witnessed ... the test-firing ... of the shells ... Was it on a Sunday?"

No answer, he was deep in thought.

"The reason I remember, I told him not to do that. I told him to take the gun to the Crime Lab.

"Holy Toledo! We're going to need a bigger boat."

After nearly five seconds or more of me sitting there wondering how the hell I was going to get out of there, I said

"...Well ..."

After another five seconds of silence, I still could not formulate a response.

Tommy Floyd had just told me, he was with Phillip Howard when the test-firing took place.

I had to say something before he realized what he had just told me. And I sure as hell wasn't going to ask him to repeat it.

After the long pause, I continued, "... the thing about Bud Kelley's statement is that Phillip Howard had been testifying in two trials that he had test-fired on Sunday afternoon."

Also, when I mentioned Detectives Phillip Howard, Dick Barnes, and Paul Robbins testified in two trials that the test-firing took place on Sunday. He interrupted me, "that (Sunday) is more significant to you! ..., than (But it didn't have anything to do with) not trying the case a third time. ..."

"Holy Toledo! Thank you Jesus, Joseph and Mary."

Sunday, November 10, 1974, was the very reason District Attorney Byron Smith backed out of the third trial and the reason Jerry Banks was freed from death row. There was no test-firing on Sunday. It was a lie.

Sunday November 10, 1974, is the most single significant phrase, date, or single point in the entire Jerry Banks trial and he just blew it off as though it wasn't a factor. I'm not saying Detective Tommy Floyd was a mushroom that had been left in the dark and I know his memory could not have been that bad. The event behind the courthouse on that Sunday was too big to forget, unless he never knew about Detective Phillip Howard's testimony about that Sunday.

Then I told him "They said they went to Jerry's house on Sunday to get the gun ... Jerry Banks said they got his gun the night of the murders when they took him in to get his statement ... but Bud Kelley said he heard the shots on Friday..."

Tommy Floyd jumped in again, "I would imagine his gun was left there (on Friday at the trailer) after he was taken home, after he was there all night."

"Exactly, they took his gun when they took him back home at 5 a.m."

Tommy Floyd said, "I remember Banks being there that night because I talked to him and I remember seeing the gun ... I think the gun was there then."

Jerry said at 5 a.m. after they dropped him off at home they took his gun. When they returned to their office anywhere before 6 a.m., it would still be dark in November. Tommy Floyd told me, he did not go back out to the crime scene with the others at 4:30 a.m. He was at the office. Jerry's gun was brought in approximately 5:20 to 5:30 a.m., when it was still dark. The test-firing would have been after the courthouse opened at 8:00 a.m. [as Tommy Floyd said, "I witnessed the test-firing, the shells that night ... or the next day, I'm not sure which."]

"Now exactly when Shug Howard fired that gun, I don't remember."

D.A. Tommy Floyd doesn't remember if it was that night or the next morning. That doesn't matter because County Commissioner Bud Kelley remembered very well.

"Well ... Bud Kelley said it was on Friday. That would be before the evidence shells were found." I explained.

"I doubt that." he said.

"Hours ... before," I added.

"I doubt that ... why would a 12-gauge shotgun be important at that time ... until ... until the 12-gauge ... it seems like those shells at the scene were found the next morning after daylight.

Ex-act-ah-mon-doe, Grasshopper! Why would Lead Detective Phillip S. Howard feel it necessary to fire a 12-gauge shotgun before the three evidence (12-gauge) shell casings were found at the scene? Which goes hand-in-hand with how did he know to use Winchester Western XX Super X 00 Buck, Mark V shotgun casing, 12-gauge.

I'm still acting as though I am a potted plant, studying D.A. Floyd's expression as he said. "I doubt that ... why would a 12-gauge shotgun be important at that time ...?

"...We knew they were killed with a shotgun, but we didn't know (at that time) if it was with a 16-gauge or a 20-gauge ..."

Now if I could have had a few minutes with him, I could have explained why old Shug Howard felt it was so important to fire those three rounds before he went to the crime scene and how he already knew that type (the manufacture, Winchester Western) 12-gauge shell casing would be needed.

Sgt. Tommy Floyd watched as Detective Howard fired that gun with the understanding that those shells were going to be sent to the Crime Lab.

Sgt. Tommy Floyd said he told Detective Howard that he should just send the gun to the Crime Lab.

From my meeting with Tommy Floyd, there were several things of which he seemed to be unaware:

1. The testimony about the Sunday test-firing, which would have been when he was with the Sheriff's Department.
2. The file which Bill Hart produced was after Sgt. Tommy Floyd was with the DA's Office. His office knew about the file and all the witnesses and their statements but he didn't.

3. *He was not aware of the contents of Bud Kelley's testimony but he validated it by his version of Friday a.m.*
4. *He was not aware of Jerry's cousin, Mamian Webster, Jr., and his statement which was withheld.*

⊕ ⊕ ⊕

Too many years have passed for me to be asking anybody anymore questions. I am not sure of what I have been told or how to process it. This was the single most amazing bit of knowledge ever discovered in Georgia v. Banks. I think someone has finally told the truth when the questions were properly placed.

I had just learned that Tommy Floyd was present when Lead Detective Howard test-fired (code word for falsified) the suspected murder weapon. Rather than explain the benefits of firing the gun hours before Detective Howard went to the crime scene, where he miraculously found the first shell at the crime scene shortly after arriving there, I had had enough. This had been too much fun for one day. I needed out of there so I could put all of this together.

The question I really wanted to ask, was, "Who was the skinny officer on the force?"

On my way out I spoke out, "Well, that was real fun."

⊕ ⊕ ⊕

That night my wife noticed I was troubled. "Are you afraid someone is going to kill you?"

"No, it's just that my meeting with Floyd did not go as well as I had hoped."

I'm glad she asked because it gave me a chance to vent and put all the pieces together at the same time. I shared with her my concerns about D.A. Floyd's remarks.

At one point his remarks bordered on sarcasm, "No, I don't know anything about anyone claiming to find the bodies with him …"

"Oh yes. It was his cousin and I think it was he who took the wallet …"

Very sarcastically, "You sound like you were there."

Given the circumstances, his remark was correctly placed.

I waste no time in processing my thoughts. I'm fast on my feet and quick with my tongue.

My mind said, "No, I wasn't there, but I know things that happened and I know more than you think, a lot more."

But, I was still holding onto the position that I had no intentions of embarrassing him or asking any questions that might be inappropriate. I was fully aware of the fact that this was a very sensitive subject 37 years ago and still so today.

The fact that others around Sgt. Tommy Floyd may have acted inappropriately without his knowledge does not diminish his contribution in law enforcement in any way.

Let me put this into perspective. I served in Vietnam operating a water craft up the rivers at the DMZ supporting the 1st Marine Division out of Dong Ha. I followed orders and traveled where and when I was told. Much like Sgt. Tommy Floyd did, under the leadership of Lead Detective Phillip Howard.

I remember each and every operation as if it were yesterday, down to the last detail of what I was doing, but not the relationship of how my contribution affected or was being affected by other forces around me at the same time or even before and afterwards.

Today my son has read every noteworthy book written by servicemen in combat in Vietnam and their operations, cause and effect. He now has the ability to look down, so to speak, to see and understand the entire picture of how each individual operation played a role in the overall picture. I do not have anywhere near his perspective of the Vietnam War, yet I was there. Does this diminish my contribution of serving my country?

Then Sgt. Tommy Floyd was put in charge of the field investigation and following up on any leads that came into the department. There were many witnesses who came forward that would have helped Jerry Banks, none of which ever made it to court other than Andrew Lake Eberhardt. And if it had not been for his efforts, he would have never been there. I have the ability to look down and see and understand the entire picture because I have studied the facts.

It becomes my truest hope that D.A. Floyd will see the murder investigations of Marvin King and Miss Hartsfield in another light.

⚜ ⚜ ⚜

One last thing: During this last hearing Detective Paul Robbins was questioned on the stand by Attorney Buddy Welch in detail about any involvement he or his friend, Schug Howard (at the time this was not to be confused with Doctor Howard or Lead Detective Howard) might have had with the Klan. Paul Robbins said he had never had any involvement with that group.
After my visit with D.A. Floyd, I remembered Attorney Welch's question to Paul Robbins. I remember rereading the name and spelling it out several times on my recording device as I read the testimony of hearing. It was spelled S-c-h-u-g. Schug Howard was a new player or was he? District Attorney Tommy Floyd referred to Lead Detective Howard as "Shug" Howard. That was what they called him. It was pronounced "sug" as in sugar. When Buddy Welch questioned Paul Robbins, the court recorded it as Suhug. I returned to my notes to put two and two together. Could it be that Attorney Buddy Welch was asking if Phillip (Shug) Howard and Paul Robbins were racist? Why would he ask something like that?

CHAPTER 25

My Journey's End

One last reply to all those who asked, "Why are you doing this? What is the need in your digging up the past? Everyone knows what happened." As I completed my work, I could not help but feel, in some way, they all might be right.

I decided to track down the victims' families. I spoke with a family member of Miss Hartsfield and explained that I was writing a book about that day in 1974 and the following events. I explained it would be best if we didn't meet each other or they know my identity. All of Marvin King and Miss Hartsfield's families still fear the unknown.

"My reason for calling you is because there is one thing that I must know before I finish. I would like to know how you and Melanie's parents have felt all these years about the way the trials unfolded and especially any feelings about Jerry Banks."

They were all in agreement. "Mr. Charles Hartsfield and his wife are now in their seventies. They can't talk about it."

My contact explained. "For 37 years they have lived with the knowledge of the brutal death of their beautiful daughter. To make matters worse, they have had to live and deal with the pain of knowing that the man responsible was set free."

That is as close to her words as I can remember. Since Jerry Banks' release from death row in 1980, not one person has explained to them the real reason Jerry Banks was released from prison.

After carefully considering the problems of bringing up the past again to another family, I located and placed a call to Marvin King's son. He told me "Don't ever call here again. How do I know if you are not going to kill me, too."

After feeling bad for about a week, I called again hoping, with his caller-ID, he would not answer. I was right, he didn't answer. I apologized as I left a message explaining I was not a danger to him. I briefed him about my concerns, my beliefs, and my reasons for the book.

He returned my call and we had a very informative conversation. He, too, had been questioning the murders and the outcome but not enough to make noise about it. His main concern was then, and still is, to protect his mother. I asked him "If I could show that it was proven years ago that Banks did not kill your father, and that the killers are still walking the streets of Henry County, wouldn't that be something you would want to know about, especially if I could point you in the direction of the guilty parties?"

He said "This is something my mother needs to know about. I am going to talk with her and call you back." Within a few days we talked again. The family thought the book was something out of their control. I had promised to respect their loved one. Therefore we agreed to move forward. They asked that I be responsible and respectful as to the use of the crime scene photograph which I told him I had. I had explained the mountain of evidence in those photographs that would make my case.

Mr. King said "We know you have a right and we cannot stop you from using the photographs but you did ask for our permission anyway. I cannot say either way if we might make it a legal issue later. He asked for their privacy in the future and he wished me luck with the book and I thanked him for that. I told him I would respect their wishes.

✥ ✥ ✥

Please follow the carefully worded statement below made on December 22, 1980, by Asst. D.A. Harold Craig and published in Atlanta papers. You will come to a better understanding of the frustrations and sorrow I have carried for the last 37 years. His words to the news reporters stir the many emotions within me that have driven me all these years.

These statements, released the next day, were pretty much all that the County would admit. (And people wonder why I felt it to be important to write about this matter.) "Mishandled evidence ...may have mishandled crucial evidence ... He (Asst. D.A. Harold Craig) emphasized that there is no evidence that Howard did tamper with or mishandled the evidence, only that the opportunity was there."

There was not one mention of the dozen or so witnesses who did not testify even though the Georgia Supreme Court felt the lack of their testimony was important enough to determine that Jerry Banks had never received a fair trial, in either the first or second trial. The District Attorney's Office fell far from the mark of telling the truth that day and left citizens in the Metro Atlanta area and far beyond thinking Jerry Banks was just another killer, who some defense lawyer helped set free on a technicality. Asst. D.A. Harold Craig failed to mention that the GBI changed their thinking about the possibility that Jerry Banks' old shotgun had been the murder weapon.

I will now share a few quotes from the last editorials in regard to Jerry Banks. The first was front page above the fold, by Linda Field and Tony Cooper of the <u>Atlanta Constitution</u> dated December 23, 1980, one day after Jerry was released from death row and three months before his death.

> "Jerry Banks, a Henry County truck driver who spent six years in prison after twice being convicted and sentenced to death for the shotgun slayings of a high school bandleader and a young woman, was released from jail Monday because prosecutors now believe a policeman may have mishandled crucial evidence.
> "Prosecutors said they will not seek a third trial.

"Banks said in an interview late Monday night that he has no ill feelings toward any of his accusers and is ready to begin life again. He will go job hunting soon.

"Henry County Assistant District Attorney Harold Craig said prosecutors recently learned that former County Chief Detective P.S. (Lead Detective Phillip) Howard may have had an opportunity to substitute shotgun shells from Banks' weapon for shells found at the scene of the killings.

"We then made the decision; we decided that we could not legally or ethically call this man (Howard) and vouch for his veracity. He had the opportunity, and we didn't want to risk putting a man on trial, based on this, with a death penalty.

"Assistant District Attorney Hal Craig emphasized that authorities have no proof that Lead Detective Howard mishandled the shells, but he said Howard had a record of mishandling evidence while employed by the Morrow Police Department.

"It was 3:30 p.m. Monday (December 22, 1974) when Banks' lawyers went to the Henry County jail. Banks said he did not believe that he was finally set free.

"'I wasn't sure at first. It kind of stunned me,'" he said as he sat in his home surrounded by friends and relatives. "'It still hasn't sunk in yet.'

"'I like Henry County. I was born here and raised here,'" he said, adding that he would begin job-hunting Monday morning.

"The one thing Banks said, he has been wanting to do is attend church. His belief in God, he said, was the main reason he survived his ordeal and why he has no anger towards any of his accusers.

"'I couldn't sit here and tell you that I believe in God and say that I'm angry at anybody. We're all human. We all make mistakes.'"

"Banks said the support of his family also strengthened him while in prison."

My Journey's End

✣ ✣ ✣

The next day, December 24, 1980, the last editorial was written by now-retired Editor Hal Gulliver.

> "The Jerry Banks Case:
> "After spending six years behind bars, Jerry Banks has finally been freed in connection with the death of Clayton County band director and one of his former students. Banks was tried twice, convicted twice and sentenced to die twice. Each time, however, the Supreme Court of Georgia overturned his conviction.
> "No one can repay Banks for the six long years he wasted behind bars. Prosecutors decided not to press for another trial on the grounds that a policeman may have mishandled the evidence. It is a pity that authorities in Henry County did not suspect earlier that their case was flawed.
> "We are pleased that Banks has been freed. But the ends of justice have not yet been met, and the Banks case raises some serious questions about official acts in Henry County. If Jerry Banks is not the killer, then who is? Why was evidence, apparently mishandled, evidence that linked Banks to the crime scene?
> "We hope the prosecutors who had the good sense to free Banks will turn their attention to finding the guilty parties and getting some straight answers about why Banks was apparently railroaded on the basis of shoddy evidence."

✣ ✣ ✣

This was the end of the murder case for the King and Hartsfield families. It was over. Of course, the death of Jerry and his wife was the icing on the cake for those who were in charge of the ***official*** *acts in Henry County*. It was really over then. You have just read the words and feelings of editor, Hal Gulliver. You have heard my same feelings expressed the day I learned of Jerry Banks' arrest on December 11, 1974, and that I have been expressing throughout this book. Nothing has changed, not one finger has been lifted to answer the first question. "*....the Banks case raises some serious questions about official acts in Henry County.*" That one statement justifies the controversial title of Jerry Banks' story, Sins of Henry County. Jimmy Glass was not where the buck stopped. For this to be allowed, it had to go much higher. There is no telling how many other lives were destroyed.

If it sounds like I have developed an attitude, give yourself a blue ribbon. I have lost the ability to discern if I am more upset over what these people did to Jerry and his entire family or if I am more upset about the fact that, for the last three decades or more, no one cared enough to ask why they got away with it. It has always been my intention to prove Jerry Banks was telling the truth and people within the Sheriff's Department were lying. I personally will not be satisfied until the FBI or the GBI investigates how those people violated Jerry Banks' civil rights and then I want the murder case of Marvin King and Melanie Ann Hartsfield re-opened as an active cold case. The reason why this has never happened is because they would have been investigating themselves.

Years ago, after Jimmy Glass was removed from office, the Henry County Police Department was formed which relieved the Sheriff's Department of their police duties and pretty much left them running warrants and being jailers. I have the utmost respect for both departments. But I needed someone I could talk to who was an outsider.

Years ago while in construction, I had the pleasure of contracting some work from an FBI agent and his lovely wife. In 2011, I called this agent and explained the problem. I was not feeling safe speaking about this case to just anyone in law enforcement in Henry County. It wasn't that I didn't trust them; I didn't trust their old retired friends with whom they might come in contact. After all, Detective Paul Robbins just retired in 2007.

He explained this would not be an issue for the FBI. He told me it would be a GBI or a local issue. After convincing him again, I truly did not know who to go to inside Henry County he gave me the name of a friend I could trust.

This FBI agent put me in touch with a detective with Henry County Police Department who he knew well. We had a very interesting conversation and I gave him a copy of my manuscript with the understanding that he would read it as a person interested in reading non-fiction crimes and not as an investigator. After he had finished reading my work, we had a private conversation off the record.

⚜ ⚜ ⚜

I have interviewed so many people over the years in my research and yet I have met few who could recognize me if I were standing in front of them. They wouldn't know me from Deep Throat's Daddy. There is one person who I never had a chance to meet. If I had known he was ill and dying, I would have made more of an effort to arrange an interview with him. He was Jerry Banks' lawyer, Attorney Stephen P. Harrison, who also maintained a law office within earshot of the courthouse. Due to his illness, I never received a reply to my queries, and wrongfully, I felt ignored. It troubled me to hear of his passing in 2010. All I have from Mr. Harrison to convey to you is his statement in response to Henry County's Assistant District Attorney Hal Craig and the others who were responsible for the official acts in Henry County in regard to Jerry Banks. It was given in an interview with Sandy Hodson, a staff writer for the Augusta Newspaper and posted on the web September 22, 1997.

> "I met him (Mr. Banks) in 1977 and began working on the case, Mr. Harrison said. The new lawyers got a tip that they should talk with a former officer working security at a community college.
> "He let us see his copy of the investigative file and in there we found all these statements, Mr. Harrison said.

"Statements in the file, including at least one by a law enforcement officer, were from people who happened to be near the wooded area where Marvin King and Melanie Hartsfield were murdered on Nov. 7, 1974. All reported they heard several gunshots fired in rapid succession. Anyone who fired the gun Mr. Banks carried that day - a broken, single-action shotgun - knew it could not have fired those shots, Mr. Harrison said.

"Sheriff's officers had withheld the name of the motorist who backed up Mr. Banks' claim of finding the bodies. Officers also withheld statements by witnesses who heard the fatal gunfire, shotgun shells found near the scene of the killings, and the name of another suspect who happened to be a law enforcement officer, Mr. Harrison said.

"This was information known to the police at both of these trials, Mr. Harrison said. If Mr. Banks' original attorney had had the money to thoroughly investigate, Mr. Banks might never have been convicted, Mr. Harrison said.

"Constitutional rights are not technicalities. It makes my blood boil when people talk of technicalities, Mr. Harrison said."

※ ※ ※

I hope by now you are convinced to some degree, Jerry Banks was not the killer and that he was framed. This was proven by three outstanding Attorneys and I have only delivered the story. If this is the case, then my job is done. If you feel there was a murder conspiracy element involved, then I hope you feel a portion of anger by knowing some of these people still walk the streets of Henry County, Georgia. If you're not convinced, then I can only offer you my closing comments and hope for a public outcry.

I found what I thought to be the end of my writing on August of 2011. I was as satisfied as anyone could be considering my limited skills, lack of access to knowledgeable people and the time and memories that have been forever lost. I often pray for Jerry and I often pray for all of the victims as a group. On August 7, 2011, I drove to work at Home Depot across town. I decided to pray for Melanie. At this point, she was the only one who could help me. My prayer started out as I asked God to forgive her for all of her sins and to please elevate her position and bless her soul. I also greeted Melanie as I closed in prayer and told her that I needed to know who and why.

While at the Home Depot, two days later, on August 9th, I passed the front entrance and noticed an officer of the law walking toward the door. I stopped and waited for him to enter because he stood out from all the other policemen for some reason. You see, I have been questioning police officers from other counties for years, trying to track down the Colliers, the father and son policemen who witnessed the four gunshots while they were at the landfill in Stockbridge the day of the murders. I had heard rumors that the son had joined a police department in one of the other counties around this area.

I asked, as I always did, "How long have you been in law-enforcement?"

When he responded "over 30 something years," it was like my cork went under water. Not only did he personally know both of the Colliers, he said, "I worked with them years ago ... I started out in Henry County under Jimmy Glass ... Oh yes, I remember [Detective] Paul Robbins well."

He knew them all. I briefly explained what I was doing and he shook his head and said, "Don't do it ... You're messing with the wrong people."

By this time I realized Melanie had held up her end of the bargain and there was no way I could ever back off now. At the risk of losing my job, as I was being paged repeatedly by management, I doggedly questioned this officer through the entire store. Wherever he shopped, I shopped! This high-ranking officer went on to explain how a certain small group of individuals were under pressure to do what they did.

And yes, he named them, at least two of them.

"No, no," I said. "They started framing him before the sun came up the next morning; they didn't have time to be under any pressure yet."

He said. "No, you don't understand. They were under pressure from others to have Marvin King and the girl killed."

This officer talked until I got light-headed with other things I had heard for years but never had anyone validate. He went on, even though he said he didn't want to get involved, and explained that there was a secret-underground-good-old-white-boy network made up of very powerful people.

"You don't want to mess with these people. They were very powerful lawyers, big executives from ..."

"Were there any judges?" I interrupted.

This man put his head down and shook it. "I'm not giving any name but yes. There were judges."

This group was very powerful and very secretive. They had access to property off of Highway 155 on the other side of the Expressway, the old Southern Railway Training Facility. They met there. It was their hideout, used for gambling, drugs, and they brought in prostitutes from Atlanta.

Was it money owed or just protection of the group's existence that Marvin King and Melanie had to be killed?

And speaking of drugs, "Were they bringing in drugs before 1981?" I asked.

"Oh, Lord, yes. That had been going on for some time." He gave me by name the person who first started bringing in the drugs to south Atlanta. He was in the loop.

As this same police officer walked away, without any more questioning on my part, he turned and said, "They even killed Billy Payne. After Jerry was sentenced to die Officer Billy Payne had grown a conscience and started drinking heavily. They were afraid he was going to talk, so they took advantage of his drinking and ran over him one night. They left him dead on a bridge. They framed another man for rape and sent him to prison also."

My Journey's End

And it is the good-old-boys who I fear, not Tommy Floyd. District Attorney Tommy Floyd could repeat my name to anyone in this good-old-boy group without Floyd knowing they or a past family member had been involved in the activities of the past.

✣ ✣ ✣

As I come to the end of my journey, I can't help but feel depressed. An editor for the <u>Atlanta Journal</u> feels the Jerry Banks story may not be of any interest to their readers. So I'm hung out to dry with no support. I have been told by this editor for the <u>Atlanta Journal</u>, Mrs. Brody, and the FBI that it will take a public outcry for this to be investigated.

When all is said and done, if anything happens to me, please don't let my efforts fade away. There are unscrupulous individuals walking the streets of McDonough, Georgia, who have gotten away with more than murder and it is the unanswered Sins of Henry County that has been the driving force of this book. I do honor Jerry Banks. I make notice here that his civil rights were taken away. I now understand why the King and Hartsfield case was never reopened in Henry County. They deserve better. It was all a dog-and-pony show orchestrated by a secret-underground network. Just because this is not the first time something like this has happened is no reason to ignore it. To me, there are still so many other unanswered questions and my work is far from over. I once thought this case would be re-opened. I truly believe the only way we will ever see that happen is by you, the readers and those of you who know the truth but have been too afraid to step forward.

Since 1974, Jerry Banks, Marvin King and Melanie Ann Hartsfield have become such a large part of my life, they have become part of my DNA. I originally wanted to stimulate people to speak out and ask who and why. Now that my journey comes to an end, I ask, do you care?

I have often asked myself, which of the two, Jerry Banks or Mamian Webster Jr., made the correct decision that day. Well under the circumstances, Mamian may have made the correct decision, but it was Jerry Banks who chose to do the right thing. He just did it in the wrong county.

To Be Continued ...

EPILOGUE

My Promise to Jerry Banks

Today in our fair town, Judge Wade Crumbley is now Superior Court Judge. My first contact with Judge Wade Crumbley came late in my writing and research out of respect for his position. I wanted to know all there was to know about this case from every aspect and from everyone else available before approaching Judge Wade Crumbley and our District Attorney, Mr. Tommy Floyd. This would limit surprises during our interview. I didn't want to take their time and then uncover other details which would require follow-up talks, further taking up their time.

Judge Wade Crumbley still feels the Jerry Banks case was the most important case of his life. He told me that he had turned down several book and movie offers. He was reluctant to give me much information at first because he wanted to protect Jerry's family.

"Enough people have been hurt already from the time of the murders on up until Jerry's convictions and even after his death."

I did not push that point but I told him, "I don't care who gets hurt from me writing this book, other than Jerry Banks' family." That was my firm statement at that time. However, as I researched Marvin King and Melanie Hartsfield, I became very protective of them and their families as well.

I explained to Judge Wade Crumbley that Jerry's case had been a part of my life since 1974, and I was bothered by the fact that not one citizen I ever talked with ever knew the truth about Jerry Banks, including his own children and other family members. I explained to the Judge I wanted to clear Jerry's name and this was something I was going to do.

If it were true, Jerry learned he was losing his wife; that would have been the biggest loss of his life. He could have found many ways to kill himself, while in prison during his six-year stay but he chose otherwise. Anyone who would shoot Melanie Hartsfield in the head with a 12-gauge shotgun could not have any type of feeling for another human being, not even a wife. I described Jerry's death earlier as from a broken heart. If Jerry did take Virginia's life, and then commit suicide, it would have been the loss of Virginia, and his children more so, than the gun shot that really killed him. One caused the other. Right or wrong, it was Jerry's feelings and the fact he had them ... feelings. That is what I'm talking about.

I have written about some real low-lifes here and let's not forget Carl Isaacs or Paul John Knowles. I cannot imagine, in my wildest dreams, any one of them having a heart or any kind of feelings anywhere near what Jerry Banks exhibited.

I would take the likes of Jerry Banks over any of those who railroaded him, any day. I would be mighty proud to have had Jerry Banks as a personal friend.

When I think of Jerry, I often think of him with his little puppy. When I see Jerry in my mind's eye, I see him working his way through the woods with a little dog. I see a young man more interested in training his puppy than he is in hunting. It takes a kind heart and a special person to love and care for a puppy. I see him standing there alongside the road, controlling his puppy so it wouldn't get hurt as he proudly waited for the police to come.

The next thing I see is a caring person. "I can't just leave them there, on the ground like that. I have to do something," Jerry told his cousin Mamian.

I see a person not concerned with white or black, it didn't matter. He cared about the victims and he cared enough to do the right thing.

Loyalty comes to mind in its greatest form by protecting his cousin even if it meant going to the electric chair. I see a young man doing his civic duty by stopping cars along the side of the road and asking strangers to call the police. I most assuredly see a loving father. It was Jerry's overwhelming love for Virginia that brought him to his knees. But it was a handful of people who got their hooks into him who destroyed a total family.

I once believed that I might get to see Jerry Banks in the afterlife and with your prayers, I still hope I can. Jerry Banks has been much more than a small part of my life since the day I first heard he was arrested. It was not just an event I heard over the radio. It was more like a vision in my head. I don't want to start something I can't explain, but I did see Jerry in my mind's eye when he was arrested. I know more about Jerry Banks than anyone, other than my wife and children and grandchildren. Jerry Banks is a part of me that will never go away, and there is nothing on this earth that will change the way I feel about him. He's like family.

We would have been about the same age today. These days, I am in my 60s. I am a white man and our grandchildren would be close in age. I was 26 and Jerry was arrested four days before his 24th birthday.

I know that Jerry is aware I care and that he will never stop entering my thoughts. There are people who say Jerry Banks will never go to Heaven. People say it is their belief that when people take their own life, they cannot go to Heaven. If that is so Jimmy Glass, Phillip Howard and others committed the sin of all sins for they took a man's soul and destroyed it, not only by what they did but by what they failed to do. If this is true, they separated Jerry Banks from his soul and from God. I cannot imagine a worse sin in the eyes of God.

I'll always pray that God will make an exception in Jerry's case.

I am a Roman Catholic and a member of St. James the Apostle Catholic Church in the beautiful city of McDonough, Georgia. For years, I was taught that when a person takes their own life, there is no forgiveness. It is an act of rejecting God, as though the person turned from God rather than turning to him. It is a way of saying God is not the answer, he can't help you. What good is he? It is said that these actions show a lack of faith and a walking away from the only power that can do all things.

God has been a part of this story from the beginning. Take the three outstanding lawyers. They were young in those days, but they were the professionals and just as sure as I'm sitting here now, I know they were sent by God. For the same reason I have prayed over the years as to what I should do. What is my role?

Now most people would answer, "Don't you think it's a little too late?"

The one thing I never stopped thinking about was Jerry's relationship with God. Jerry was gone and there was no bringing him back. So why was Jerry always in my thoughts? One day I realized that proving Jerry Banks was framed was only part of his being on my mind all the time. I realized, a more important mission was to pray for his soul and this became my passion. I want you to understand the importance of praying for all the victims, but more so for Jerry because of how he left us. Some will never truly believe Jerry Banks died the way the Sheriff's Department report claimed. I can accept and understand either cause of death. The main issue is, it is so essential for anyone with an ounce of compassion to pray for Jerry Banks' soul.

Over the years, I have learned that there are still a lot of old school teachings still in our everyday lives. I have also been raised to believe that only God knows your soul and he and only he has the last word.

One Sunday morning, I spoke briefly with our priest, "Father John, I have some concerns about your, and more importantly God's, teaching on suicide."

After assuring him that I was fine and there was nothing to worry about with me, he agreed to meet with me privately to discuss this matter.

We have a few things in our church that are different from others and one thing is Purgatory. Now I'm not going into who's right or wrong, just believe in what you believe in, and live it. I just need to explain so you'll understand the importance of my new dream. Let me do this by asking a few questions. Let us say that when Mother Teresa of Calcutta died, did she go to Heaven or Hell? You guessed Heaven and you are correct. Did she have any difficulty getting in? No, you again guessed correctly.

Now I'll let you pick the must villainous person ever born to this earth and, without judging of course, run that person through the same set of questions. Let's say just for the sake of making a point, this person went to Hell.

Don't feel guilty, you haven't sent anyone anywhere.

Now let's look at Jerry Banks. Only God knows what went on between Jerry Banks and God during those last tormented minutes from the time he saw Virginia and the time he hit the floor. Only God knows what Jerry's mind was put through over that six-year period. Jerry Banks loved God. God said he will never give you more than you can bear. A sound and healthy mind can handle more than a broken mind. There is the possibility in the brief moment in time before and after he pulled the trigger, that Jerry cried out, "Forgive me. Dear God ..."

Now run Jerry through the same questions. No, he did not go to Heaven and yes he could have gone to Hell. But, if God forgave him, where does he go? Jerry Banks by far was not the most villainous person and he certainly was no Mother Teresa. God never wants to lose a single soul to Hell. In fact, I have it from a highly reliable source that God does not send anyone to Hell. Everyone stands in the presence of God when your time comes, and standing there without the human ability to lie. God asks you "what do you deserve?" It is the way and manner in which you chose to live here on earth that this decision is made. You freely make the decision by the way you live here on earth and you make it again as you stand before God.

It's like this: Mother Teresa was allowed to enter the Kingdom of God because her feet were clean. The other guy, the one you chose ...well, let's say, his feet were not cleanable. My friend, Jerry and I, we need purgation. We need cleansing. We need purifying. This happens in Purgatory. Some souls will stay in Purgatory until the end of time, here on Earth as we know it, while others will advance to Heaven much sooner.

I truly feel that Jerry is in Purgatory and he will be in Heaven some day. As a community we must offer our prayers to restore his soul. As we pray for our loved ones who have passed, they are elevated in Purgatory and during our prayers they are allowed to hear us. Now that is beautiful to me. All of this is because God does not want to lose one soul, if it can be saved.

I managed to go by the Banks family church, just north of McDonough. There was a large group of people inside the meeting hall and as I walked in, I interrupted them by asking if anyone knew any of the Banks family. One of the ladies said "yes" and she stated that they were ending their prayer group and they would be finished shortly. I was standing outside when the flood gates were opened and I met two dozen of the sweetest ladies and truly nicest gentlemen as nearly all of them were family members of Jerry's. They were all near Jerry's age, if he had lived, or a little older ... cousins, aunts, and uncles. I do not recall many not being family and not one person who did not know him and Virginia. They also led me to find Jerry and Virginia's grave site. It saddened me deeply to finally know the place just below my feet was where Jerry was buried. I was as close to him as I would ever get on this earth. A calm relief came over me as I learned for the first time that Virginia Banks had been placed at Jerry's side. This was an extremely thoughtful and caring act of the Lemon family. Until then, I was under the wrong impression that they had buried her elsewhere in the Lemons' resting place.

I mentioned there were several reasons I wrote this book. It is my dream to have a special service in honor of Jerry and Virginia Banks as well as Marvin King and Melanie Ann Hartsfield. Jerry Banks, his children and this community need this significant prayer service. It's about forgiveness for all, Jerry's sins, the community, the Sins of Henry County.

In the words of Saint Teresa of Calcutta: "You cannot do what I do, and I cannot do what you do, but together we both can do beautiful things for God."

Learning all that I could about Jerry as a person over these years was inspiring. I now think back to when this all started, and I thought Jerry was on my mind because he needed my help. That he was crying out for me to solely help him. I found out quickly, before I could help save Jerry's soul, I would need to do some house-cleaning first. I have needed Jerry as much as Jerry needed me.

The Church teaches us the best time to pray for the souls in Purgatory is on the date of their death, their birthday, and the date of their baptism but anytime will elevate them in their position in Purgatory closer to God. Jerry Banks was born on January 18, 1951, and he died on March 29, 1981. I have no knowledge of his baptism at this time.

As for me, if this case is not reopened and these people are not made to answer for what they have done, I'm a dead man! I only ask that you let the authorities know justice has not been served. Thank you for reading Jerry Banks' story.

Contact the Attorney General of Georgia
Mailing Address:
Office of the Attorney General
40 Capitol Square, SW
Atlanta, Ga. 30334
Phone:
(404) 656-3300
Fax:
(404) 657-8733

LIST OF MAIN CHARACTERS

(*Those whose whereabouts are unknown, are unknown to me*)

Jerry Banks: Arrested December 11, 1974. Found guilty January 31, 1975. Found guilty again November 18, 1975. Released on December 22, 1980. Died on March 29, 1981.

Officer Jerry Banks Jr.: DeKalb Police Officer Jerry Jr. is living in the Atlanta area. Jerry Banks Jr. told me once he left Henry County, he never set foot back here.

Mrs. Banks: Jerry's mother passed away at 89 on July 3, 2011. Her headstone gave her name as Nannie L Banks. She was buried alongside Jerry and Virginia Banks.

Perry Banks: Brother Perry Banks still lives in South Atlanta.

Ed Banks: Son of Jerry Banks Sr. lives in the Atlanta area.

Felicia Banks: Daughter of Jerry Banks Sr. is married and lives somewhere in McDonough.

Det. Charles Richard (Dick) Barnes: First officer on the scene. Testified during both trials that Det. Phillip Howard's test-firing was on Sunday, November 10, 1974. He also testified he talk to Eberhardt. Whereabouts unknown.

Police Chief Hershel Childs: McDonough's Chief of Police and government witness in Jimmy Glass's drug trial. Still lives in McDonough.

Assistant D.A Harold Craig: Assistant Prosecutor during the 2nd trial. Whereabouts unknown.

Judge Alex Crumbley: Jerry's lawyer after Hudson John Myers. He has his law practice a block south of the courthouse square.

Judge Wade Crumbley: Jerry Banks' lawyer. Presently Superior Court Judge of Henry County.

Andrew Lake Eberhardt: The motorist who Jerry flagged down. Whereabouts unknown.

Kelly Fite: GBI Ballistics expert. Retired.

Sgt. Tommy Floyd: The arresting officer of Jerry Banks. Tommy Floyd is still the Henry County District Attorney as of 2012.

Detective Mark Foster: Friend of Marvin King, Narcotics Detective from Griffin, Georgia and onetime suspect in the murder. Believed to be living in Panama City, Florida.

Sheriff Jimmy Glass: Sheriff of Henry County, 1973-1981. Served time in Federal Prison for importing drugs. Still living in McDonough, Georgia.

Sgt. Johnny Glover: Discovered Marvin Kings' car one mile from the murder scene. Still living in McDonough. Retired.

Mrs. Carrie May Hambrick: Dear friend of Jerry Banks. Mrs. Hambrick passed way in January 2011, very close to Jerry's birthday. May God bless her soul.

Hardrock: Friend of many. Passed away 2011. His real name….

Attorney Stephen P. Harrison: Jerry Banks' lawyer. He had a law office one block from the court house as of 2010 in McDonough. Mr. Harrison passed away in 2011.

Officer Bill Hart: Found the third shell on December 13, 1974. He turned over a file containing "withheld evidence" to Jerry's new lawyers. Passed away from heart attack.

Bill Hinton: Drug trafficker and airport operator. Died in prison approximately 1982 or 83.

Doctor Howard: Head of the GBI Crime Lab and State Medical Examiner. Performed the autopsies on the victims.

Lead Det. Phillip S. Howard: Did he falsify the shell evidence and lie under oath about test-firing on November 10, 1974? Did he withhold evidence in two trials? Would it matter if Jerry's lawyers suspected he was a KKK member? Some say he is dead.

Commissioner Bud Kelley: Witnessed the test-firing of Jerry Banks' shotgun on the morning of November 8, 1974.

Kelleytown, Georgia Wikipedia: Bud Kelley served as a Henry County Commissioner from 1969 to 1976. Under his capacity as a

List of main characters

commissioner, Bud helped influence the idea of building Henry Medical Center (at the time, many in the community thought the notion of building a hospital in Henry County as unnecessary and too expensive). Bud Kelley is credited with improving race relations in Henry County and, in 1972, appointed the first African-American to serve on the County Planning and Zoning Board.

Robert A. (Bob) Maddox: My dear friend. Passed away January 23, 2011.

Retired Detective Keith Martin: Clayton County Detective involved with finger printing and polygraph testing. Practicing Attorney in Clayton County and a very nice individual.

District Attorney Ed McGarity: Prosecuted the 1st and 2nd trial. Passed away. His son Judge Arch McGarity is the Chief Judge at the very same court house. Judge Arch McGarity was helpful in allowing access to photos without a court order.

Defense Attorney Hudson John Myers: Jerry's lawyer during the first and second trials. Rumor has it he was run out of town and later disbarred. Whereabouts unknown.

Sgt. Billy Payne: Was in the loop but played no active role in either trial. He was murdered and left lying on a bridge, crossing I-75, south of McDonough, Georgia.

Det. Paul Robbins: Testified in a death penalty trial that Lead Detective Phillip Howard test-fired Jerry Banks' shotgun on a Sunday, November 10, 1074. Lives in Henry County.

Detective Ted Ray: Found the second evidence shell the morning of November 8, 1974.

Charles L. Sargent: Author. Still living in McDonough and finishing Memories Left Behind. Always looking for other projects.

D.A. Byron Smith: The D. A. who wanted a third trial. Rumor has it he is a retired Judge in Jackson, Georgia.

Judge Sosebee: Trial Judge during the first and second trial. Whereabouts unknown.

Attorney Larry Tew: Probate Judge and practicing Attorney and Government witness in Jimmy Glass's drug trial. Whereabouts unknown.

Detective Charles Tomlinson: still lives in McDonough and helps Jimmy Glass to and from his doctor appointments as part of his ministry.

Mamian Webster Jr.: Hunted with Jerry the day they found the bodies. Mamian is living somewhere south of Atlanta. Perry Banks still has not found him.

Attorney A. J. "Buddy" Welch: His firm Smith, Welch, Webb and White is located in McDonough and Stockbridge, Georgia.

Miss. Willy: My first interview. I recently stopped by the church to attend services with Miss. Willy and Charles Tomlinson.

Made in the USA
Columbia, SC
16 July 2023